Praise for #1 Bestselling Author Joe Bovino's First Book, *Field Guide to Chicks of the United States*

Judge, 2013 Global eBook Awards (Gold Medal, Humor)

The illustrations were fantastic. The book was hilarious. I laughed through the whole thing (and I'm a chick ... LOL).

Tamazon, Night Owls Reviews (Top Pick)

Field Guide to Chicks of the United States by Joe Bovino is a hilarious look into the women of the USA. If you like people watching and commenting I can say you need to check this book out today. You and your friends will want to read this together for the most laughs … My husband and I enjoyed this book. For those who don't find this hilarious feel free to seek your comedy somewhere else.

Kimberly McClain Cardenas rated it 5 of 5 stars · Shelves: goodreads-wins

I won this from Goodreads.com. This is a seriously funny although fairly spot on kind of book. It is very straight forward and not for those who take offense to stereotypes. Yes even a girl like me was represented almost to a tee. I am sending it next to my brother so he can pick and choose his next girlfriend a little more carefully next time and with a lot more knowledge behind him …

Concerned citizen (APO, AE USA) 5.0 out of 5 stars – Amazon.com

Great gift for ANYONE: Enjoyed the book so much I've been bought it for the embassy Marine guards here in Bangkok to help them 'transition' to the states. ANY guy is a rock star in Thailand, so I want them to have a tactical advantage. Great product Joe.

Michael Peters

This is awesome!!! I can't wait to start handing these out as gifts. When is there gonna be a Joe Bovino school of cool online education masters program?

Colleen Schilinski rated it 5 of 5 stars – Goodreads.com

This was a great book. It's funny and all my guy friends want to borrow it. I'll have to put my information on the inside of this book, so I get it back. It is a must read for anyone, because Joe Bovino did a great job telling us the way it is about woman in different city's all across the United States. I even have quite a few pages marked for future references, and to show certain men in my life. This is definitely a GOODREAD for me.

MAXIM Magazine

Outlandishly Hilarious.

Katia 5.0 out of 5 stars – Amazon.com

I absolutely LOVE LOVE LOVE the book!!! Hilarious! It's been a while since I've read something that comical ... I'm a critical person and I honestly thought it was going to be like every other book out there on women. Clearly, a well-researched product.

Baniva 5.0 out of 5 stars – Amazon.com

I'm gay and I love it! This book is so funny, I met Joe at an event and he told me about his masterpiece. I was a little hesitant at first but I decided to go ahead and buy one! It is painfully accurate as I was able to match up some characteristics of my girlfriends to their cartoon counterparts. It's the most genius thing ever. Loved it so much I bought another for a friend who I consider a connoisseur of the "female species"!

Brian Olea, On-Air Personality, Mansion Mayhem, Playboy Radio, SiriusXM 102

I thought after 16 years working at the Playboy Mansion, I knew everything about women! Joe has definitely done his research and his book has even taught me a thing or two! Proof that not all women are alike!

Abigail Ratchford ("It" Girl/Model/Actress) @AbiRatchford

@chickspotting haha so funny! I dont know if im here [in Los Angeles] long enough to agree with a lot of the statements [about the LA "Mattress" (Model/Actress) chick species profile], only moved here about 4 months ago.

xtime Past - 5.0 out of 5 stars, Amazon.com, April 21, 2015

This is one badass book! This has heavy red pill material and every MGTOW/PUA should read this. Why not learn from wisdom and the details of the American soulful dynamics. Pure fun and extensive research occurred and undertaken to bring this material to a shining light ... Reread: YES. RP/MGTOW: YES. [Rating:] 10/10. Thanks for adding smiles to our faces! Bravo!

Marissa 5.0 out of 5 stars – Amazon.com

This book is hilarious! Not to miss, easy read, light hearted and will make you laugh. Everyone might be a little thrown off at first, some maybe offended, but once you actually read it you will see the humor and love it. Not only is it a great convo starter and even better gift, but it is the written out guide to chicks ...! Read, compare and enjoy. Guys will love it and girls too ... Definitely recommend it for good laughs and fun. Find out who you are ladies and guys, your "dream" girl awaits ... Well done and I look forward to sharing this book with friends.

Arktik Fitness "Michelle" (Juneau AK) 5.0 out of 5 stars – Amazon.com

So Glad I Downloaded! Starting reading last night & was worried about waking the husband up with my laughing! Irreverent, hilarious & spot on in some spooky ways :) You've done your research Joe!

Amar B. (Chicago, IL USA) 5.0 out of 5 stars – Amazon.com

This could be considered be the greatest book ever written since the Kama Sutra. Buying this book would constitute the smartest book buying decision you have ever made.

VenusLovesVirgo @VenusLovesVirgo

Girls this is what men REALLY think of U! FUNNY A$$ BOOK! CHICK GUIDE!

Tony Bruno, Sports Talk Radio Legend

My book finally got published! ... Good job, Joe (Bovino). I couldn't resist picking it up in a men's store at MGM Grand in Vegas.

Mike B. "Cashcowz" (New Jersey) 5.0 out of 5 stars – Amazon.com

If there were a Pulitzer Prize for originality and humor, this book would be a slam dunk winner. Creative format, entertaining yet educational text, and fantastic illustrations are synthesized to perfection. Whether it's "How-to", "Has-been", or "Wish-I-could", this book is the bible for the Chickspotter in all of us - including females who should keep an eye on the competition.

Prince Billy Alexander III, Field Producer, Celebzter.com

My new Bible.

Paris Minton rated it 5 of 5 stars Shelves: first-reads – Goodreads.com

I wish I could give this book more than 5 stars. It is the funniest thing I've read in a long time, and I'm very grateful to have gotten my copy for free through the Good Reads first-reads giveaway.

Bovino has managed to creatively and thoroughly create a well-researched and colorfully written (and drawn) guide to ALL of the women that the United States has to offer. At first I was skeptical that anyone could pull this off, seeing that people are individuals and I do not support stereotypes ...

With that being said I must admit that the writing and observations are spot on! Feminists may take offense to this book, but I recommend it to EVERY man in America. It may save you from getting involved with a crazy woman, wasting time on a lost cause, or just save you from boredom. It's a great conversation piece to have around the house and show company, and as you read it you'll notice similarities between the archetypes Bovino has illustrated and the real women in your life. I enjoyed this book a lot. I crack it open whenever I need a good laugh, and I am sure you'll love it too.

Luv Lotus (California) 5.0 out of 5 stars – Amazon.com, June 17, 2014

Joe Bovino took a lot of heat from feminists for objectifying racial types. I think this book is ADORABLE. It makes you realize all the delicious variety of us women. I think Joe just LOVES all kinds of women and he celebrates them in this book. The illustrations are adorable. It's a FUN read. And it opens you to the richness of looking outside your own tribe to see that there's a richness of opportunities to date all kinds of amazing women.

Paul (United States) 5.0 out of 5 stars - Amazon.com

Where was this book when I was single? This book would have come in handy back in my single days. As it stands, it's still great entertainment to read through each description. It's a humorous look at so many dynamics of the fairer sex, written in a style that is fun and makes you want to keep reading. Cultural and geographic influences really do exist and the author has clearly spent a ton of time doing research and compiling it into a book that is both funny and educational.

Danny Hickman 5.0 out of 5 stars – Amazon.com, January 3, 2014

Absolutely hilarious and yet … very accurate!!! I received my copy yesterday afternoon and by bedtime last night, I had finished it! I'm an armchair chickspotter now and this guide definitely makes it a lot more fun! As I read through this highly insightful and very humorous look at the genus Femalis Americanis, I thought back to all of my times in the field and how handy this would have been back then.

My wife decided, after listening to me chuckling and watching me nod my head repeatedly that she needed to see what had piqued my interest. Within a few minutes, she was reading right along with me and we were comparing notes on the women we know and laughing at how accurate these descriptions are. I haven't yet decided which classification she falls under, but I'm sure my choice will elicit a spirited discussion!

Rohit Bhargava @rohitbargava

Field Guide to Chicks is offensively brilliant.

Braden Traub 5.0 out of 5 stars – Amazon.com

It's hard to do justice to a book such as "field guide to chicks" in a short amazon review, but that's the nature of a book that has so many things going for it. Not only did I find myself cracking up on just about every turn of the page, but after my laughing fits settled down I found myself coming to the realization that the material in the book is actually very accurate despite it also being absolutely hilarious!

I'll be frank here — every American man should have this book proudly displayed on his coffee table. I know that I'll be handing out several of these this Christmas and I highly recommend everyone do the same. Do NOT miss this book.

Caiti rated it 4 of 5 stars – Goodreads.com

This book was hilarious. It's not for the easily offended, but if you have a sense of humor check it out. It's written in the same format as bird watching books, which provide in depth descriptions of species, etc. The author of this book uses hilarious often local stereotypes to describe just about every flavor of female in the country. I can't wait for this book to be more widely read so everyone knows what I'm talking about when I use the author's hilarious classifications to describe people I meet in everyday life. I definitely recommend this book if you are not easily offended and need a side splitting laugh.

Dorothy 5.0 out of 5 stars – Amazon.com

I thought this book was really funny. A bit sexist, well a lot sexist, but still funny. If you are a feminist, then don't even bother with it. Kind of like a grown up version of Mad Magazine. Kind of potty mouth. But if you have a sense of humor then it's fun. My husband stole it from me and took it to work. They have been passing it around at work laughing at it.

JBad 5.0 out of 5 stars – Amazon.com

Awesome. This book was expertly written. Right on target. Fun to read. Really fun to look up where I fit in. A must have in any social circle.

James M. Starnes (ANNAPOLIS, MD, US) 5.0 out of 5 stars – Amazon.com

Fun fun read … I have had over 200 match.com dates …. and let me tell you, Joe is spot on with his observations about the types of chicks that are wandering around our great country!

Linda 5.0 out of 5 stars – Amazon.com

Love This Book!!! This is definitely a must read book … You will not be disappointed … You will not be able to put it down … He is an amazing author :)

WHY *Latinas* GET the GUY

Three-Time Bestselling Author
JOE BOVINO

SAOIRSE PUBLISHING

NOTICE

Copyright © 2015 Joe Bovino
All rights reserved

No part of this book may be used or reproduced in any manner whatsoever without written permission from Joe Bovino or his designated representative, except in the case of brief quotations embodied in critical articles or reviews.

By purchasing this book, you acknowledge and agree to the following: You understand that the information in this book is an opinion and should be used for personal entertainment purposes only. You are responsible for your own behavior and nothing in this book is to be considered legal or personal advice with regard to any specific situation or problem.

The author, publisher, and their representatives actively and regularly search the Internet for individuals who violate their copyrights, trademarks, and other intellectual property rights and take whatever action is necessary to enforce and protect them.

"JOE BOVINO," "GHOST TO GODDESS," and "CHICASPOTTING" are trademarks of Joe Bovino.

DEDICATION

To my mom and dad, who I couldn't love more.

I am one lucky gringo to be your son.

Thanks for putting up with me.

CONTENTS

Introduction 1

Chapter One: **KARMA IS A BITCH** 5
- What Goes Around Comes Around, Bitches 6
- Militant Feminism: Ain't That a Kick in the Balls 11
- Yes, American Women Really Are That Bad 16

Chapter Two: **JANE, YOU IGNORANT SLUT** 25
- Slutty Is As Slutty Does 26

Chapter Three: **AMERICA'S LATINAS:**
They're Not All Mexican, Becky 31
- Chicaspotting: Is It Really All About That Bass? 32
- 14 Subcultures of Latin-American Women
  1. Taco Belle (Mexican American) 36
  2. Bumbshell (Brazilian American) 40
  3. Euro-Mina (Argentine American) 44
  4. Symmetrical Force (Colombian American) 48
  5. Ecuadorable (Ecuadorian American) 52
  6. La Guitarra (Puerto Rican – South) 56
  7. Nuyorican (Puerto Rican – Northeast) 60
  8. Trifecta (Venezuelan American) 64
  9. Transformer (Cuban American) 68
  10. Perusian (Peruvian American) 72
  11. Cinnamon Swirl (Dominican American – Florida) 76
  12. Beauty Call (Dominican American – Northeast) 80

13. Pupusa (Salvadoran American)	84
14. Hotemalan (Guatemalan American)	88

Chapter Four: **AMERICAN WOMEN: If She Looks Like a Man, Talks Like a Man, and Sleeps Around Like a Man, She's Probably an American Woman** 93

- American Chickspotting: What You See Is What You Get 94
- 14 Subcultures of American Women
    1. 49er (San Francisco, CA) 96
    2. Sili-Clone (Orange County, CA) 100
    3. Star Burst (California) 104
    4. Perfect 6 (Seattle, WA) 108
    5. Bigger Better Deal (Aspen, CO) 112
    6. Hole in One (Las Vegas, NV) 116
    7. South Beeotch (Miami Beach, FL) 120
    8. Boca Bitch (Boca Raton, FL) 124
    9. So Ho' (New York, NY) 128
    10. Bronx Tail (Northeast) 132
    11. Hurt Rocker (Emo) 136
    12. Brooding Barfly (Hipster) 140
    13. Big Bang (Rubenesque) 144
    14. Cougar (Sexual Predator) 148

Chapter Five: **THE GHOST TO GODDESS PRINCIPLES** 153

- How to Go from Ghost to Goddess 154
- Advice for America's Latinas 171

Notes 173
Credits 179
Acknowledgments 180
Conclusion 181
About the Author 182

INTRODUCTION

> "Why is the fact that each of us comes from a culture with its own distinctive mix of strengths and weaknesses, tendencies and predispositions, so difficult to acknowledge? Who we are cannot be separated from where we're from …"
> — Malcolm Gladwell, *Outliers: The Story of Success*

In *Men on Strike: Why Men Are Boycotting Marriage, Fatherhood, and the American Dream — and Why It Matters*, Dr. Helen Smith explains why men are boycotting marriage, fatherhood, and the American dream as American women and society become increasingly hostile and anti-male. It's an outstanding book and covers a lot of territory untouched here, but Dr. Smith doesn't go far enough in her critique of American women and misses another unintended consequence of the anti-men trend.

American men aren't just taking their balls and going home. They're taking a harder look at their options in a multifaceted global dating market, concluding that many foreign and hyphenated-American women offer an appealing alternative, and rationally choosing Latinas and other warm-hearted, respectful, confidently feminine women over ball-busting, highly demanding, manlier American ones.

Truth is, notwithstanding complaints by American women who struggle with dating and relationships in today's hook-up culture, feeling unattractive, unfeminine or even invisible at times, there are still plenty of good men looking for love and marriage.

They're just not that into shrew. Or sluts, for that matter.

This book will demonstrate that Latinas appeal to men for many reasons besides their world-famous booties. And they're emerging on the scene precisely as a huge number of American women have stopped making a serious effort to compete, deluded themselves into believing that bitchiness is attractive, and bought into the destructive propaganda of militant feminism. As they say, timing is everything.

How do I know? I spent almost four years querying single men and women across the country about the most distinctive physical traits, vocalizations, behavioral tendencies, and cultural predispositions of American and hyphenated-American women during the course of researching and writing my first book, *Field Guide to Chicks of the United States*. I reviewed every published report, study, book, and online source of information I could find on the subject. I joined and studied dating websites, which commonly require users to define their ethnicity, location, and mating preferences. And, last but not least, I dated women of all kinds for decades, particularly while residing in multicultural Miami and Los Angeles.

This book will pick up where my first book left off by examining why Latinas are rocking America's dysfunctional dating scene, nabbing the country's most eligible bachelors, and leaving militant feminists dazed, confused, and alone with their bad attitudes. It will employ bird watching methodology to compare and contrast fourteen subcultures of American and Latin-American women. And, in the final chapter, it will introduce 10 *Ghost to Goddess Principles* for American women who want to turn the heads and win the hearts of America's best men by being the best they can be.

I *love* America and its women — well, most of them anyway — but some things just aren't being said that should be. Too many so-called dating and relationship experts tell American women only what they want to hear, even if it's patently false and counterproductive, and I'm tired of watching it pass for wisdom. Feminist Groupthink stifles debate, demonizes dissenters, and defies basic common sense. Most men know this and can't stand it but won't say so publicly because they don't want to ruffle the feathers of snarky, unscrupulous defenders of the status quo. It's one of many reasons no good man in his right mind wants to seriously date or marry any of them.

Do Latinas always get the guy?

Of course not. Many American guys never consider dating or marrying anyone other than a girl-next-door, even if she keeps slamming it in his face. Some men focus only on a shrinking number of American women who are approachable, kind, and ladylike, even if they have to move thousands of miles to find them. Others avoid American women altogether by dating and marrying only Asian, Middle Eastern, African or European women. But a lot of great American guys are falling for the most conspicuously sexy women on the planet, Latinas. So, that's where we'll begin.

Let's start with a few useful definitions.

Who are America's "best guys" and "most eligible bachelors?" This sizeable group doesn't include dating site trolls, true misogynists, or any man in search of a woman who doubles as a "doormat." There's no excuse for them. America's best guys love and respect women who earn and deserve their love and respect. They're *good* and *decent* men, gentlemen, bad boys (with an upside), or any other guy with potential to be an excellent boyfriend, husband or soulmate, but they're suffering from the relationship equivalent of post-traumatic stress disorder or animal cruelty from dealing with the worst of American women for so long.

"Latinas" are women of Latin-American origin or descent who identify in meaningful ways with one or more distinct Latin-American cultures, such as Mexican, Colombian, Venezuelan, Puerto Rican, Cuban, Guatemalan, or Brazilian. "America's Latinas" are Latinas who live in the United States and plan to stay — legally or illegally. They're Americanized to one degree or another, but they're not fully assimilated. Ethnicity and Hispanic culture still noticeably influence their appearance, attitudes and behavior.

Conversely, for purposes of this book, "American women" are fully assimilated American females who don't identify strongly with their ethnic background anymore. For example, a lily-white woman in Vermont whose grandparents emigrated from Germany may be proud of her Western European heritage, but her appearance, attitudes and behavior are far more likely to reflect where and how she was raised, and/or where she chooses to live as an adult, in the United States. In her case, American culture and regional subculture trump ethnicity. She's American. That's it — no hyphen.

Black women who were born in the United States often refer to themselves as hyphenated Americans — that is, African-Americans — even though they're fully assimilated American citizens in every other way. However, notwithstanding the enduring hyphen and how strongly so many black women identify with their racial group and history, the definition of "American women" herein will also apply to black women who were born in the USA. I think that makes sense under the circumstances, and I want to be as sensitive and respectful as possible about this.

This book will not assume that America's Latinas are homogenous because they're not, and they'll tell you so in no uncertain terms. (Have you ever asked a Colombian-American woman if she's Mexican? Not a good idea.) There are many obvious physical, behavioral and cultural differences between a *Euro-Mina* (Argentine-American woman) in Miami and a *Nuyorican* (Puerto Rican woman) in New York City, for example. Chapter Three will address these differences in a direct and (hopefully) amusing way.

American women also differ in observable ways from coast to coast, especially in terms of their attitudes toward men, money, and family values. And many American women still treat men with kindness, love and respect, particularly in the traditional South and Midwest. These good women aren't part of the problem — they're part of the *solution* — but they're not in charge anymore. Pugnacious feminists, manly slobs, and selfie-obsessed narcissists, cheered on by the media, have largely marginalized America's best women and drowned out their pleasant voices with a pervasive, deafening shrillness.

Who are these unpleasant women who are driving good men away and into the arms of Latinas in droves?

Chapter One tackles that question.

CHAPTER ONE

KARMA IS A BITCH

"Life is 50% Attitude and 50% ... Attitude."
— Barbara Ann Bovino (aka, "Mom")

What Goes Around Comes Around, Bitches

As I write this, the Amazon #1 bestselling book in America on dating and mate-seeking is entitled *Why Men Love Bitches*. That book, with a lie for a title, speaks volumes about American women and the sad state of affairs for decent American men in search of a good woman to date, marry, and love. It sends exactly the wrong message to American women at precisely the wrong time. It also partially explains why Latinas and other proudly feminine women who don't share that hostile mindset are in such demand.

Let's start with a dose of reality.

Here's what the word "*bitch*" actually means:

- "a malicious, spiteful, or overbearing woman" (Merriam-Webster);
- "a woman considered to be mean, overbearing, or contemptible;" (http://www.thefreedictionary.com/bitch) and
- "the worst species of woman: the Feminus Obnoxium." (Askmen.com)

Men love all kinds of women, but they don't love bitches. They don't even *like* bitches. No one does. Bitches don't even like themselves.

But that's not what America's militant feminists want you to think and believe. They need to convince other women that bitchiness is cool, smart, and somehow appealing to good men. So they deliberately mislead anyone who will listen, parrot a demonstrably false narrative, and lie if it suits their purposes.

Some delusional American women actually *brag* about being a complete bitch and then argue that it's an effective way to interact with American men.

Consider Gigi Engle. In her viral blog post on December 16, 2014 entitled "*24 Reasons Nice Guys Always Chase The B*tch – As Told By The B*tch*," Ms. Engle describes herself as a "rude" (ostensibly white) "Alpha Bitch" with a "huge ego" who "says the meanest things" and "horrible things" to "perfectly nice guys," who respond "like sick puppies" to her "black widow ways" and "bitch-tastic glory." Yep, according to Ms. Engle, she's a nice-guy magnet because she treats all men like sh*t.

Ms. Engle goes on to claim that "ultra-sweet" American guys are "obsessed" with her and other "nasty," "bossy," "volatile," "complex," "elusive and difficult" Alpha Bitches who are "uninterested in what anyone else thinks," "have very little attention and time to devote to [men]," and act like "a complete a-hole." That's right, according to Ms. Engle "in some "f*cking twisted" way, these desperate yes-men and "mamas' boys" actually enjoy being "babied and … abused," "second-in-command" and "slapped around" by bitches from hell. She sums it up this way: "In the end, the nice girls get cats, the boys get their hearts broke and the huge bitch gets the corner office and a martini."

Lovely, isn't it? Ms. Engle probably doesn't care that almost everything she says and believes is wrong, but it is. She and other "Alpha Bitches" are repulsive to any self-respecting guy, not just alpha males. Whether they know it or not, they appeal only to pathetically weak men (who should know better) and normal, horny guys who are willing to tolerate their disgusting personalities, appearance and hygiene long enough to get laid, shower up, and leave. You see, bitches like Ms. Engle may be hard to stomach for more than a few minutes, but they tend to mirror the wildly promiscuous behavior of the same male jerks and players whom they profess to hate.

Sherry Argov, the New York Times #1 bestselling author of *Why Men Love Bitches: From Doormat to Dreamgirl — A Woman's Guide to Holding Her Own in a Relationship*, is coyer than Ms. Engle, but the destructive impact of her book on gullible American women is far greater.

Rather than encourage women to embrace bitchiness for what it is — pure nastiness — Ms. Argov, like a good propagandist, distorts the plain meaning of the word "bitch" beyond all recognition. At one point, she even goes so far as to define a "bitch" as her polar opposite: A nice girl. "A bitch is *nice*. She's sweet as a Georgia peach. She smiles and she is feminine." Then she adds: "Let us conclude … by redefining the word *bitch*. Think of it as a "term of endearment."

Bitch, please.

Even Ms. Engle, as vile as she is, manages to be honest about the nature of an American bitch and deserves some credit for it. Ms. Argov, not so much. She begins with this whopper in the introduction of her book:

> "Among the hundreds of interviews I conducted with men for the book, over 90 percent laughed and agreed

> with the title within the first thirty seconds. Some men chuckled as if their best-kept secret had just been revealed."

Excuse me? What woman in her right mind believes that load of BS? The opposite is true, and I don't need a poll to figure it out. Men love women who are sweet and highly feminine, among other things, not bitchy or manly. Polar opposites attract. That's why over 90 percent of men will tell you that they avoid bitches like the plague. The rest are morons or need a hearing aid.

Misleading American women into believing that men secretly love bitches is bad enough, but Ms. Argov doesn't stop there. She encourages her readers to become a "High-Maintenance Bitch," as if it's some kind of an achievement:

> "The only higher crown, the only higher honor, is to be called a "High-Maintenance Bitch." It's a sign of success, indicating that this is the woman the guy ends up keeping. If nothing else, he keeps her for the very practical reason that he's invested so much that he can't let her go."

That is truly barf-worthy advice. No man wants to attract, get or keep a high-maintenance bitch, and it doesn't take a rocket scientist to know why. Is it any wonder that guys are looking for more appealing alternatives when so many misguided American women actually believe this drivel?

By this point, you may be saying that none of this matters because Ms. Argov is surely just kidding around. She's using the word "bitch" in a playful, tongue-in-cheek way to mean something vaguely positive, you might say, like a strong, independent woman, a nice girl with a backbone, or ... whatever. Well, I can appreciate attempts at humor even in a cringeworthy "relationship guide for women" like Ms. Argov's, but shouldn't men be in on the joke? She apparently doesn't think so:

> "If that fateful day ever does arrive when he tells you that you are a bitch? Stop, and take a deep breath. Then enjoy the moment. Smile internally as you say to yourself, 'Okay. Now I know he *truly* does love me.'"

Uh, no. When a man calls a woman a bitch, he's using the plain meaning of the word, not Ms. Argov's meaningless redefinition. That's nothing to smile about.

Then Ms. Argov really exposes herself.

What should American women who are "too nice" *do* to become a bitch-who's-not-really-a-bitch? Well, of course: Think, talk and act more like the *dictionary* definition of a bitch — that is, more like Ms. Engle.

Yep, after all the word games and inside jokes, Ms. Argov's new bitch is the old bitch.

- A bitch "understands — and adheres to — the first law of nature: Every animal for herself." (Give me a f*cking break.)
- "Just remember, it isn't about a man … Do things when it is convenient, especially if it regards your relationship of choice and who you let in on the 'inside.'"
- "The bitch never tries that hard to make an impression."
- Women should develop "irreverence … for what other people think" because a bitch "doesn't try to live up to anyone else's standards — only her own."
- "The bitch … gives a very different message. 'Who I am is enough. Take it or leave it.'"
- "A woman … demeans herself when she compares herself to another woman."
- "Any time a woman competes with another woman, she demeans herself."
- A woman shouldn't "kill herself to impress anyone."
- A woman shouldn't cook for her man because cooking is "one of the many ways that women overcompensate." (Now she's really pissed off the Latinas, and rightly so.)
- "Being sassy means you won't knock yourself out."
- "A bitch doesn't rely on [a particular miniskirt, a belly ring, or a black dress with a plunging neckline] to feel good about herself. She relies on *who she is as a woman*." (This is envy masked as advice.)
- "If he tells [a bitch that] he doesn't like red lipstick, she wears it anyway, if it makes her feel good."
- The bitch should "throw a little weight around" and "put him in his place once in a while …"

Translation: Screw him. Screw her. Screw them. Screw everybody! Do whatever the hell you want and men will find you irresistible. WRONG.

Here's the problem with that horrible attitude: There's no "reverse magnet" for bitches in the real world. Women who believe the big lie can't compete with Latinas and others who make an effort to look, speak and act in ways that men actually like and admire. They also unwittingly set themselves up for disappointment, loneliness and defeat. America's Latinas are playing to win … and will kick their flabby, entitled, selfish butts to the curb.

Latinas are rarely wilting flowers or "doormats," as you may have noticed, but they're smart enough to know that men don't love manly, indifferent, self-centered bitches. And unlike Ms. Engle, Argov, and other delusional American women, *they don't equate femininity with weakness*. They enjoy being sexy, highly feminine women and realize that respect and love from men is earned, not a birthright or unconditional entitlement.

American women who make dumb mistakes with men — like dropping all of their friends or any semblance of a life of their own — need some new habits, but bitchiness isn't one of them. There's no need to dress, talk or act like a man, either. It's unnatural and highly likely to backfire.

What about women who do all the right things but still aren't treated well on a date or in a relationship? That's easy. Move on. If a man really cares about you, he won't allow you to feel like anything other than a goddess for any extended period of time. Nor should you let him. There are plenty of great guys out there looking for a girl with some self-respect, a healthy attitude, and her eye on the ball.

I gave the same kind of tough-love advice to my two younger sisters, and they ended up marrying fantastic guys. It works — even for the nice girls.

Militant Feminism: Ain't That a Kick in the Balls

The role of militant feminism in damaging gender relations in the United States and driving good men away from American women cannot be overstated. I'm not referring to feminism that seeks to ensure that women receive equal justice under the law, which I wholeheartedly support. I'm referring to the most insidious version, with its laser focus on American male-bashing at every turn. It has become mainstream and incessant over the last few decades, especially if the guy happens to be white.

America's anti-men trend is arguably most pronounced and vicious online. And, in that respect, one of the worst offenders is Jezebel, a snarky feminist website known for blog posts that portray (American) men as idiots, creeps and criminals, unless they shut up or do and say only what's politically correct.

In *"Watch a Woman Experience 100 Instances of Street Harassment in One Day,"* for example, Jezebel's Kara Brown writes indignantly about Shoshana Roberts, who was filmed using a hidden camera as she walked along the streets of New York City for 10 hours amid catcalls, comments and other unappreciated attention from men, including one black guy who followed her around for five minutes. Ms. Brown laments that this type of "exhausting sexism" and "day to day bullshit ... can really wear on your spirit." Indeed, according to Ms. Brown, all of this "shitty male behavior" constitutes "street harassment" that is "goddamn infuriating, frustrating and at times terrifying" and must be stopped. Here's how she so delicately puts it:

> "[T]o be clear, all of it sucks ... from the innocuous, 'Hey, what's up girl,' to the man who, after she ignored a 'compliment' yelled: 'Somebody's acknowledging you for being beautiful. You should say thank you more.' *Sir, fuck your compliment and fuck your entire existence on this planet.*"

Charming, huh? What man could resist her?

Then Ms. Brown goes on to share a truly harrowing and "degrading" experience of her own while shopping at a flea market in Los Angeles a few months ago. Some clown had the audacity to try to get her attention and spark a conversation by saying, "Hey beautiful." Oh, my God! It was war. She couldn't take it anymore:

"I quickly snapped: 'My name isn't fucking beautiful.' The man who had yelled at me came closer and said: 'I just wanted to let you know that I think you're beautiful.' I said: 'I don't give a fuck what you think.' … A few minutes later that same man approached me to apologize. He said he wasn't trying to holler at or bother me, (lies) but just wanted to give me a compliment. I told him that my self-esteem is not dependent upon the affirmation of strangers and he should stop doing that shit to me and other women."

Fortunately for the poor guy who didn't notice that big chip on Ms. Brown's shoulder, she didn't kick him in the balls, too. In "*How to Kick a Guy in the Balls: An Illustrated Guide,*" Jezebel's resident ball-busting expert, Susan Schorn, recommends a swift, hard kick in the nuts for any man who puts a woman in a threatening situation. "To attack a man's testicles is to attack his identity, his virility. It also, so the rumor goes, hurts like holy hell," she says. Ms. Schorn acknowledges that it's "[p]retty ugly" when it happens, but she doesn't "feel sorry for men" because "[i]t's more than a fair trade, running the world, even if you have to keep one hand over your crotch at all times."

If I ever meet Mses. Brown or Schorn, that's where one of my hands will be.

Of course, there's no excuse for truly threatening behavior toward women, including stalking Ms. Roberts for blocks on a public street, which was way over the line. I get it, but let's be honest: Ms. Roberts walked around for *10 hours* in some dicey NYC neighborhoods in a tight t-shirt, hoping that guys would notice her so that she could secretly film it, edit the video down to *2 minutes*, and make all men look like creeps.

I wouldn't have bothered speaking to a woman like Ms. Roberts in that situation, and neither would most of my friends, but that doesn't make it wrong to do so. Most of the almost exclusively black and Hispanic guys who did try to engage or connect with her said something innocuous or complimentary, got no response, and gave up. And, while shouting "Damn!" when a hot woman walks by isn't my idea of a good opening line, it's not an insult, and I'm sure it works once in a while if it evokes a laugh or a smile.

As for Ms. Brown, she's an embarrassment. Bitter, short-tempered, foul-mouthed women like her tarnish the image and reputation of American women worldwide and make it harder for the best ones to receive the love, attention and respect they otherwise deserve. They're also extremely selective in their sexist outrage. Handsome guys like Tom Brady never get called out for doing much worse than the average Joe. (Watch Mr. Brady at work by Googling "Sexual Harassment and You.")

Latin-American women are used to receiving compliments and attention from men and rarely freak out when it happens. They expect to be noticed when they enter a room, walk down the street, or go to the grocery store because they normally make an effort to look as attractive as possible wherever they go. Most Latinas in Miami won't even leave the house without looking like a million dollars, and they genuinely appreciate it when others acknowledge their beauty in a friendly, non-threatening way.

Latinas don't waste time walking around with a hidden camera looking for trouble either. They've got more important things to do … like meeting a nice guy at the flea market.

Unfortunately, as you'll see in the next subchapter of this book, the same American feminists who complain about sexism and a "rape culture" when men pay attention to them in a remotely sexual way whine even louder when guys ignore them. It's maddeningly hypocritical, but it doesn't surprise me. I know from firsthand experience just how sleazy the unwashed, basement-dwelling feminists of Jezebel can be.

Yep, believe it or not, my first book inspired two of the 100 most popular Jezebel blog posts of 2014 — without attribution, of course.

Here's what happened in a nutshell:

In late April of 2012, four months before my first book, *Field Guide to Chicks of the United States*, was printed or available for anyone to read, my former publicist decided to write a little blurb about the book and distribute it to her contacts. She asked me not to edit her work because publicists have their own way of doing things, and I agreed. Big mistake.

To my amazement, *without reading a single word* of my book, Lindy West of Jezebel published a blog post on May 8, 2012 entitled "*The 92 'Species' of Women According to an Incredibly Stupid Dude from a P90X Video.*" The very next day, Emma Grey of Huff Post Women piled on with a blog post of her own entitled "*Joe Bovino's 'Field Guide to Chicks of the United States' May Be Worst Book Ever.*" That's right, Ms. Grey hadn't read my book either but thought it might be worse than *Mein Kampf*.

In November of 2012, a little over a month after the *Field Guide* was released and began to garner praise from actual readers, I wrote to Mses. West and Grey and offered to send them a courtesy copy to read and, hopefully, review again. Ms. Grey ignored me. Ms. West, on the other hand, wrote back to say that I seemed like "a good sport" and she'd be "happy to give it a shot!" and possibly even engage in a "genuine dialogue" on the subject. I was delighted to hear from her and looked forward to that dialogue, but nothing happened for over a year.

Then, in February of 2014, after I stumbled upon another blog post by Ms. West about how it feels to be fat, hungover and obnoxious on a plane, I sent her another message. This time, suspecting that she still hadn't opened my book, I provided a link to excerpts that I'd recently posted on my website. All she had to do was click and read.

Ms. West didn't respond or write another review of my book. Instead, she apparently decided that Jezebel should copy my concept as closely as possible without getting sued, and she got one of her colleagues, Erin Gloria Ryan, to do the dirty work. Sure enough, on April 2, 2014, Ms. Ryan published a blog post entitled "*The United States of Bros: A Map and Field Guide,*" which ended up as one of the "*100 Most Popular Jezebel Posts of 2014.*" It's a shameless, painfully unfunny rip-off of my copyrighted work, which Jezebel supposedly hated, without attribution.

And she wasn't done. On June 30, 2014, Ms. Ryan followed up with "*The United States of Basic Bitches: A Map and Field Guide,*" which also became one of Jezebel's 100 most popular blog posts of 2014. It didn't include any mention of my book — or Ms. West's May 8, 2012 post trashing it, either.

The whole episode was unethical, hypocritical, possibly actionable, and sadly typical of militant feminism today.

On the bright side, if imitation is the sincerest form of flattery, I should be flattered.

Now you know the rest of the story …

Online nastiness like this from Jezebel, Huff Post Women and other snarky feminist outlets sullies the image of American women, worsens gender relations, and accelerates a disturbing anti-men trend, but it pales in comparison to the damage that militant feminism does in the real world each day. We see it all the time, and 2014 was a particularly destructive year.

How bad was it? Even the liberal LA Times published a blog post by Charlotte Allen on December 19, 2014 entitled *"Top 10 feminist fiascos of 2014."* According to Ms. Allen, the 10 worst feminist blunders last year included:

1) The "gang rape" hoax at UVA; (As a proud UVA alum, this disgusts me.)

2) Wendy Davis; (Wendy Davis who?)

3) Rotherham; (U.S. feminists fail to respond in a meaningful way to the *"real rape culture"* perpetrated mostly by British-Pakistani men in Britain "because the perpetrators weren't the white middle-class men who are feminists' preferred villains.")

4) #Shirtstorm; (That poor bastard)

5) Hobby Lobby;

6) The Nine West shoe store ad ragefest;

7) The Great Spider-Woman Sexiest Derriere Scandal;

8) F-Bombs for Feminism;

9) Amanda Marcotte; and

10) "Ban Bossy." (Feminists love to ban sh*t, including words.)

That's a solid list, but let's not forget Lena Dunham's false rape accusation; pasty white Elizabeth Warren's dubious claim to be 1/32 Cherokee, which led Harvard Law School to promote her as their first "woman of color;" and the muted feminist response to kidnapping, rape and sexual enslavement of women and girls by Boko Haram and ISIS.

What a mess. Life is hard enough without delusional American women making things worse, especially if you happen to be a white guy who's less than 1/32 Cherokee.

Bring on the Latinas.

Yes, American Women Really Are That Bad

In *"No Sex in the City: What It's Like to Be Female and Foreign in Japan,"* American blogger and globetrotting feminist, Reannon Muth, opened Pandora's box by failing to understand why she couldn't get laid in Japan and taking no responsibility for it.

According to Ms. Muth, within a few weeks of her arrival in Tokyo, she was "mysteriously, frustratingly invisible." And it stayed that way for the rest of her nine-month stint as an English teacher there:

> "Most days I felt unattractive, unwanted and worst of all, unfemale. When not even a short skirt or slinky top attracted more than a passing glance and even construction workers, who could usually be counted on for a leer, regarded me with bored, blank expressions, I felt like a Martian. And very, very alone."

To make matters worse, her male expat counterparts were living like rock stars, easily hooking up with model-thin Japanese beauty queens.

Naturally, she blamed and belittled the men for not noticing, dating, and having sex with her, as if they'd shirked their job responsibilities. Japanese men "were in fact attracted to" her but were "too intimidated" to speak with "the Jennifer Anistons of the expat world." They super-secretly desired her but couldn't handle an American woman as "strong, independent, assertive and outspoken" as she was. She was "virtually un-datable" because she was just "so different, so foreign," and so *awesome*, not because no one actually wanted to date her. Meanwhile, "[d]orky," "socially awkward" expat men, also known as "White Dudes" and "white boys," were even less interested. They "flat-out ignored" her.

It didn't take long for Ms. Muth's more sensible readers to pound her with the raw, unfiltered truth: American women like her need an attitude adjustment. Badly. Everyone knows it but them.

Incredulous and defensive, Ms. Muth published a follow-up blog post entitled *"Are North American Women Really THAT Bad?,"* which elicited another brutally honest response.

Here are some of the most telling comments, starting with one from a Latina who got the guy. This one really hits home:

Irene:

"I am a Colombian girl studying in the US, back in Colombia and while I lived in Europe, I was able to make many connections with women; I am straight but women were always open to me being a woman and actually trying to be friends. It's here in the USA where women according to my experience tend to be ABSOLUTELY AND TOTAL BITCHES!! Sorry but I have never been exposed to such megalomaniacs, competitive, bitchy, angry, psycho, fake, plastic women in my entire life!!! ... I have NOT had a problem finding dates in America, in fact I found my fiancé here, an all American boy from Wisconsin who treat me like a princess, but guess what American women ... I EARNED THAT RESPECT AND LOVE. In my country you to stay in shape, I wear dresses, skirts, make up because I ENJOY BEING A WOMAN ... women here don't understand the concept of [femininity] and think [femininity] = weakness. For example I love cooking, my mom taught me to cook because it's a mother-daughter bonding thing in my culture, and guess what? I cook for me and my American boyfriend, to the point he now wants to learn how to cook ... good luck finding an American girl who can cook, most of his friends dating American women just get Chinese or pizza while the slob of an American girlfriend sits there in her [pajamas] waiting for the food delivery to arrive while drinking beer ... women have been nothing but evil towards me, and it's because of how I dress, of how I act, they assume I am being fake and [pretentious] but this is who I am ... I can sense a deep sense of jealousy in them because they think that by me being feminine and enjoying catering to my man, I am being a fake girl! Let's not even talk about sex, American women have so many hang ups and think Sex is a tool to control men ... it's pathetic but I was branded as a slut because I said I enjoy pleasing my man and being pleased by him. NO WONDER AMERICAN WOMEN OVERSEAS HAVE SUCH A DIFFICULTY FINDING MEN!"

Tiago:

"Here in Brazil we view American women as good for sex and bad for love."

Jackie:

"If you want to see how bad [North] American women are — come sit in a divorce court. I've worked for years there and though it troubles me to admit it I have to say American women are by far the nastiest creatures I come across in my work. Half the time they just want the kids to hurt the husband and the other ha[lf] they want the money to hurt him and don't at least pretend to care about the kids. Unless women in this country stop drinking of the poison well that is man hating feminism (no I'm not talking about equal rights feminism of course) they better start learning to enjoy their cats. I see a lot of women with cats. Lots and lots of cats."

Joe (who evidently married a "High-Maintenance Bitch"):

"I'm married to one of those ultra shallow, no good, lazy, American women. I find NOTHING good about them in general. American women are gross and unladylike. They are greedy and extremely self-centered … If I could find a way to unload this rotten bitch I'm with now and get a foreign girl, I'd do it in a second!"

divemedic:

"In my travels, I saw the same thing from a male's perspective, and I have a slightly different take on it. The problem is that American women are known the world over as being self-centered and demanding princesses who feel like men should be kissing up to their posteriors. Not so in Europe, and most assuredly not true in Japan."

Brent:

"What's been going on in the economic sector provides an excellent allegory for what's happening in the dating world right now. Western women have figuratively "priced themselves out of the market" much like what happened with organized labor in the United States and Canada. As the world is becoming more globalized, western women no longer need to fear competition from Susie down the street, but also from some other women halfway around the world. Oftentimes these women are thinner, better looking and still raised with traditional family values instilled in them. Most women overseas are happy and grateful to receive the affections of a well-educated western man from a good family ... I predict that the demographic changes that will occur in the next 20 years will be astounding."

Slim:

"So basically some chick goes a few months without getting laid and has to write a snarky deprecating blog entry attacking white dudes? Huh? If you can't get laid in Japan that is YOUR problem, not the fault of guys you deem to be below your standards. Rather than lashing out, your time would be better spent on improving your own negative attitude. Also, if you were really as good looking as you claim you are, I'm sure that the Japanese men wouldn't be fleeing from you like an ornery white she-[G]odzilla."

Bob:

"The only reason American men date/marry American women is out of sheer ignorance. It just never occurs to most American men, living in the cocoon of American culture, that FAR better options are available. I have never met an American guy, who has dated an Asian or Eastern European lady, and then decided afterward that [he prefers] Americans. It doesn't happen. EVER. Getting away from American women is akin to finally waking up from a lifelong nightmare that you didn't realize you were in. The only hope American women have is that most American men remain insulted and ignorant of the fact that women from anywhere else on Earth are better, in every conceivable way, than their American counterparts."

George:

"Maybe some men value the sloppy-dressing, shrill, judgmental, obnoxious pseudo-men most American women have become … Your lazy, high-minded opinions on the treatment you believe to be entitled to have no value to the majority of men on planet earth. Americans are stuck with you. We are not … We (men) are just sick of being criticized & told what to do by women who haven't earned our respect. Any man who tried same would get punched in the face. But you're a woman. So we marginalize you. We ignore you. That's why we won't date you. That's why we won't marry you."

Vin:

"I can comment on American women – particularly women in San Francisco, where I live. Friends and I joke about it a lot; the women here don't try very hard in the dating game, but expect the world from guys … I'll just use dress as one of many examples. Women in San Francisco dress like crap. They wear torn up Converse All Stars and old jeans. A hot girl can pull that off, but you have to be incredibly hot. SF women generally aren't up to that standard, and come across as lazy, entitled slobs. All you have to do is visit London, Tokyo, Seoul, Hong Kong to see the drastic differences between women – the effort they put into dating, and how they present themselves as opposed to N. American girls. I always joke with my friends that American women should be shipped off to Seoul for a couple years after college to be humbled. ha ha."

Shane:

"The fact is that women in North America need an attitude adjustment BADLY and the arrogance and conceit shown by "[Reannon]" are exhibit A in the case of common sense vs. the irrational and demanding white woman. She spent 2 blog entries and a total of 6-8 pages whining about how nobody wanted to put up with her nonsense overseas. SURPRISE! In a dating environment where men aren't forced to put up with rich little white girl nonsense, they typically don't choose to put up with rich little white girl nonsense. Mind blowing stuff, I know."

Anonymous:

"The difference between the US and Europe is the way that women's rights have developed over the past 50 years and the decisions that were made to do that. In the US women saw men as having more rights and decided that they wanted to be more like men. In Europe women simply wanted to have the same rights and opportunities as men but did so without trying to take on masculine traits. This is why European women retain their femininity whereas American women see femininity as being from an era when they were treated as second-class citizens."

hmm:

"As a foreign guy, I must say that I'd never marry an American woman although they're great for some quick fun. I've seen friends marry AW and suffer through emasculation, adultery, divorce, and loss of children and worldly possessions …"

Alex:

"The value that Western women believe they possess compared to what they can actually offer a man is so out of whack, it's laughable. The men who avoided you overseas did so because for the first time in their lives, they had a choice … I blame this failing on our parents' generation more than anything else. I believe that when women won the right to get a divorce, it was intended to be used sparingly to extricate themselves from horrible situations and abusive relationships. Now it seems to be used when a women gets bored, finds a richer guy or [wants] to fleece men of half their belongings."

John:

"It's fifty million times worse for men in America. Why do you think we go abroad? Because we get treated like sh*t in our own countries unless we're mega rich or male models."

Allan:

"I have traveled all over the world conducting multi-billion dollar business, and American/Canadian women are valued about as much as a homeless man in New York City. They are viewed as feminazis, narcissistic, histrionic, materialistic, shallow, and useless … Generally speaking, American women make the worst WIVES, but are known for being great for CASUAL UNATTACHED SEX."

Andrew:

"In my years of business travels in Eastern and Central Europe, Middle East, Asia, and South America, in my years of talking with my friends who have been working and living in these countries, I have to say that it's in America where the dating rules defy all logic or evolutionary laws. In America, after graduation and college years, the dating scene is so bad, and I mean really bad, that they had to come up with online dating sites and speed dating. Really? Do men really need to fall so low, in order to find a date online or go to a speed dating event and jump from table to table every 5 minutes looking like an idiot. And at the end the chances to find a date is close to zero. I have never seen in my life where US men fell this low. It's pathetic. A man should have no difficulty to go on the street, sees a nice lady and ask her phone number and meet her later for drinks. This should be the norm and easy. But if a man with good manners, clean cut, well dressed with a good paying job regularly gets rejected, then I have to say that there is something very wrong with women in US. Something is wrong with the female mind set. And based on your article that I have read, I can see why …

However, in other countries, people don't need to go [to] online dating sites or speed dating because women are easy to approach, easy to ask out and most of the cases, they will say yes. In America it's just the opposite. Most of US women will automatically say no, like a robot, even if you are good looking, good manners and educated …

Here is the real kicker. Men from other countries are well aware of the dating situation in America. People talk. Men talk. And they are well aware of how bad US women can get when it comes to asking them out ... Ladies, you don't have a good reputation at all ...

Why should any guy in Japan, or Thailand or Russia or Brazil or Poland even bother to approach you when the first thing that will come out of your mouth is NO. They are not interested [in feeding] your egos."

Energy Law:

"Honestly, it's because you American women look like livestock in high heels when surrounded by Japanese, Korean, Turkish, Polish women. And your extreme abrasive bitch personality doesn't help. So stay in those "bubbles" they call the USA or Canada. I teach English in Armenia, and your fat American white asses wouldn't get any attention here, either!"

Randomperson:

"I personally think western women are very decadent. I blame feminism; it teaches women they are god's gift to earth and don't have to do anything to earn respect and that the world owes them everything. It teach American women that they need to be accepted for who they are and to ignore male needs. That's why 70% of American women are obese.

I'm [an] eastern European male who lives in the US, and when I go back to [E]astern Europe, the treatment I get from women is completely different. They actually respect me as a man and don't try to turn me into their personal servant.

American women on the other hand believe I owe them the world. It's actually a serious problem. The marriage rates in the US are at their lowest point. 80% of divorces are initiated by women. America's legal system is stacked against males.

I hope western women realize that their idea of equality is one sided or else western society will collapse."

Hans:

"American women. The most entitled creatures on the planet. And even when reality takes you by the neck and shoves your noses into your sh*tty attitude you manage to blame everybody else for being nothing but horrible partners to men. You may laugh at the nerds you're feeling so much better than. But they will get laid and make money for their new families while you will end up as cat ladies when the bad-boy c*ck carousel throws you off for the new hot tweens. Karma is indeed a bitch. Love it."

To be fair, notwithstanding her condescending attitude toward certain men, Reannon seems like a relatively nice young woman, and I respect her willingness to travel and experience different cultures. Her blog posts weren't completely baseless, either — cultural factors surely played some part in her inability to get laid in Japan — or nearly as snide as the daily rubbish from those back-stabbing bottom-feeders at Jezebel. But I bet she's still in denial about the problem with American women and the opportunity it presents for Latinas and other confidently feminine women to get and keep the guy.

By the way, as it turns out, one of my younger sisters is happily married to a great Japanese-American guy. Yep. Some American women — the cream of the crop — know how to get and keep a great guy wherever they go.

The rest should think twice about claims by militant feminists that men love bitches. They just don't. (No one does.) They don't love sluts, either, for anything besides hookups and other sexual "transactions." The best American men are looking harder than ever for something and someone else, as explained more fully in Chapter Two.

FREE NO-BS DATING & RELATIONSHIP ADVICE

This book is INTERACTIVE.

For free access to more no-BS advice, training videos, and book updates, visit **JoeBovino.com**.

CHAPTER TWO

JANE, YOU IGNORANT SLUT

"A lady doesn't wander all over the room, and blow on some other guy's dice."

— Frank Sinatra, *Luck Be A Lady*

"Miley Cyrus defended her VMA performance by saying she made history. So did the Titanic, but only 2,000 men went down on her."

— Joan Rivers

Slutty Is As Slutty Does

Dan Ackroyd used to begin his counterpoint presentation on the "Point/Counterpoint" segment of the Saturday Night Live Weekend Update by looking at Jane Curtin and saying: "Jane, you ignorant slut." It was hilarious. Google it and watch the video (again) for a laugh.

So relax, ladies. I'm not referring to you … unless of course you are, in fact, an ignorant slut. Or even just kind of slutty. Then, we should talk. That's not the way to get the guy. Latinas know this. You should too.

I don't want to sound like a killjoy, and I'm not suggesting there aren't exceptions to the rule, but this is a book about why Latinas are getting the best guys, and the cold, manly way that so many American women sleep around these days is one of those reasons.

Why is the shameless promiscuity of American women such a big deal?

Since this really isn't that complicated, I'll cut to the chase:

Men lose respect for women who sleep around or have sex too quickly, especially on the first date. That's just the way it is. Guys will deny it to get laid or suck-up and feminists will deny it to supposedly "empower" women, but it's true. And nothing good happens in a relationship when a man loses respect for a woman, particularly in the long-term. Once he starts to think you have sex at the drop of a hat with this one, that one, and the other one, he already has one foot out the door.

So how long should a woman wait to have sex with a new guy?

Refrain for at least a month in most cases. That's how Latinas normally roll and, as Tony Robbins likes to say: "Success leaves clues."

Many American women use the so-called "three-date rule" to justify banging any bloke who's still standing after three dates. Big mistake. And trying to avoid responsibility by blaming men for the rule is lame. Women have always been in charge of how long it takes to go from zero to 60 when it comes to sex. Guys just go along for the ride.

The three-date rule works against the interests of American women for three main reasons. First, many gullible women figure that, since sex is right around the corner anyway, they might as well have it on the second date, first date, or even after just meeting a guy (for a one-night stand). Pressure builds not to wait for even three measly dates and just go for it ... like a man. It happens all the time.

Second, it's too easy for a douchebag to send out his best representative for a few dates, tell an impressionable woman what she wants to hear, and end up in her pants. I've seen it a thousand times. My dad once said: "You don't really know a man until you've seen him angry." Do you really know how a new guy handles his anger by the end of the third date? Probably not.

Third, men simply won't respect or like a woman (as much) if she's having sex on automatic pilot with every guy she dates. If she acts like sex with her is nothing special, so will he.

When I moved from Los Angeles to Miami in 2005, it didn't take me long to figure out that Latinas were playing by another set of "rules." They were usually as sweet as can be, dressed provocatively, and sexy as hell even by high LA standards, but they were *different* — in a good way — and they made it clear by their words and actions. Sure, some were more promiscuous than others (especially in the trendiest South Beach nightclubs), but the hottest and most desirable Latinas wanted plenty of time to figure out who I really was and what my intentions were before anybody got naked.

One night in a trendy bar in Brickell (the financial district of Miami), I asked a handsome Latin guy whether the 3-date rule applies to Latinas. He just laughed and told me that most Latinas will wait at least a month to have sex with a guy after the courtship begins. I didn't mind. The risk-reward ratio worked in my favor. Yes, the risk of getting no action for an extended period of time was greater, but so was the possibility of a relationship with a beautiful, highly feminine woman who had enough self-esteem not to give it up to any guy who threw down a few bucks for three dates. Count me in. The only guys who didn't like it were the jerks who couldn't fake it for a month or more.

Sherry Argov, author of *Why Men Love Bitches*, also advises women to wait at least a month to have sex with a new guy. She deserves credit for reaching that conclusion, but not for her logic. Ms. Argov thinks it's all about power, not love or romance. "Most men are turned on by a bitch because it's a thrill to take down a powerful woman," she says, and a smart bitch "keeps her power in *every* way." Women should act like cold, manipulative bitches when it comes to sex because men perceive "an emotional woman as more of a pushover." Wrong again, Sherry, and you just insulted millions of Latinas.

We're not talking about a business transaction or prostitution here. We're talking about dating and relationships, where bitchiness serves no purpose.

Latinas tend to be more emotional than American women. Does that make them pushovers? Hardly. Anybody who says that knows nothing about them.

Here's an uncomfortable truth: Privately, many Latinas will tell you (as they told me) that American women are gross and embarrassing because they have sex like men. It's practically man-on-man, they say, and it's disgusting to any self-respecting Latina. Worse yet, this "open legs" policy has fueled an American hook-up culture where horny guys think they can hit (it) and run. That makes dating more difficult for everyone else.

Latinas may look, walk, and talk sexy, and many are incredibly passionate in bed, but that doesn't mean they're acting like anything less than a lady when it comes to dating and sex. Most of America's Latinas outside of New York City (where they unfortunately tend to pick up bad habits of American women more quickly) make a guy wait and work for it. They give men enough time to f*ck-up by hitting on another girl, throwing a temper tantrum, saying something stupid or disrespectful, not calling or being sufficiently attentive, or otherwise not making them feel like a princess.

But what about the guy who gestures toward his crotch with a pained expression after you pull away and says something like "Now, what am I supposed to do with this?" It's not right to leave him like that, is it?

Short answer: His blue balls aren't your problem. It's a pathetic attempt to guilt you into finishing the job and should never be taken seriously. I can't believe that American women ever fall for this ridiculous ploy, but some do. Teasing is fair game, no matter how long it goes on without sex. Guys who think they've found a keeper will wait as long as it takes.

So ... how do you know if a woman qualifies as a slut?

Slutty is as slutty does.

There are certainly shades of grey on the sluttiness spectrum: Not slutty, occasionally slutty, classically slutty, extremely slutty, and so on. There's also a big difference between *acting like* a slut on rare occasions and *being* a slut all the time. Fair enough.

But let's be honest: Highly promiscuous women who sleep around like men know they're sluts. So does everyone else, including the guys they "date."

Some American women delude themselves into believing that they're not slutty by redefining the word into something vaguely positive (e.g., liberated, empowered, assertive) or using the tired "double-standard" argument — if men can do it, so can women — as justification for the sluttiest behavior imaginable. Nice try. Men see right through it.

Others convince themselves that sluttiness is OK — even ideal — as long as it's done right. There's actually a book called *The Ethical Slut: A Practical Guide to Polyamory, Open Relationships and Other Adventures* by "[e]xperienced ethical sluts Dossie Easton and Janet W. Hardy." (Their children must be proud.) According to Amazon, customers who bought that trash also bought *Why Men Love Sluts*; *Think Like a Man, Act Like a Slut*; and *The Ethical Ho*. (Just kidding, but the books they did buy were almost as bad.)

Will *some* men choose to date or marry a slut? Yes, I suppose — for a while at least. There's no accounting for taste.

But American women who want a great guy should get their brakes fixed and start pumping them — not him — harder and more often. Otherwise, don't be surprised when the only men who stick around are jerks, players and hapless beta males. The best guys can do better. And, since many of them have turned to America's Latinas, that's what we'll do in Chapter Three.

LET'S HOOK UP!

Like what you've read so far?

If so, join my beautiful friend and me for some free training videos, livecasts, no-BS dating and relationship advice, book updates, and more.

Visit **JoeBovino.com.**

CHAPTER THREE

AMERICA'S LATINAS:
They're Not All Mexican, Becky

"In the post-Cold War world flags count and so do other symbols of cultural identity, including crosses, crescents, and even head coverings, because culture counts, and cultural identity is what is most meaningful to most people."

— Samuel P. Huntington, *The Clash of Civilizations and the Remaking of World Order*

Chicaspotting: Is It Really All About That Bass?

In my first book, *Field Guide to Chicks of the United States,* I employed the techniques and methodology of arguably the best and most enthusiastic observers of nature in the American field — birders — to profile 90 subcultures (or "species") of American and hyphenated-American women. I called it "*chickspotting,*" a variant of two of the world's most popular pastimes, *bird watching* and *people watching.*

This observation-based approach made sense for three reasons. First, unlike most books and articles about women and relationships, mine stuck to the facts. Instead of trying to determine *why* women behave as they do or look a certain way, it examined *what* they do and *how* to spot them when they do it. Second, by keeping it pithy, illustrated, and easy to read two pages at time (on the john), I stood a better chance of getting guys to read it, not just their girlfriends. Third, I thought it was funny. If I couldn't write a book that was insightful *and* entertaining, I wasn't interested.

This chapter will apply the same bird watching techniques and methodology to the study of America's Latinas, also known as "*chicaspotting.*" You can't fully understand the allure of chicas in the United States until you can distinguish between the species. Nevertheless, as far as I know, no one else has ever bothered to make those distinctions in a book like this.

Then, in Chapter Four, I'll do the same thing with some identifiable subcultures of fully assimilated American women. If you don't notice any striking differences between American and Latin-American women after perusing all of those profiles, you're not paying attention.

Some of my critics insist that every woman is unique (or the same) and any attempt to analyze or categorize women by group or subculture is offensive, sexist, and wrong. Others claim that practically all such generalizations about women perpetuate harmful stereotypes. And some say that merely using the word "chicks" or "chicas" objectifies women, even if it's clearly just a good-natured play on words.

These are legitimate concerns. It's undoubtedly true that inner beauty is what really counts with people — unlike birds — but let's not put our heads in the sand. Anyone can see that the American field includes a wide variety of women.

Consider the Italian American *Guidette,* for example. Early drafts of my first book included a profile of the *Guidette* subculture long before MTV aired its "Jersey Shore" reality television series. She was relatively unknown to most Americans back then, but I grew up in Jersey and knew her well. Now, almost everyone knows more than they care to about the *Guidette* and her male counterpart, the Guido. Did MTV make Guidettes like "Snooki" and "Jwoww" famous by identifying a stereotype, a subculture, or both? That question led to big controversy — and bigger ratings — for MTV, but one thing is clear: A *Guidette* subculture exists and many people find it fascinating ... in a train-wreck sort of way.

Cultural and subcultural strengths, weaknesses, tendencies and predispositions, like distinctive physical traits, distinguish us from one another in meaningful ways, and there's nothing wrong with acknowledging it.

The 14 chicas profiled in this chapter are as follows:

1. Taco Belle (Mexican American)
2. Bumbshell (Brazilian American)
3. Euro-Mina (Argentine American)
4. Trifecta (Venezuelan American)
5. Symmetrical Force (Colombian American)
6. Transformer (Cuban American)
7. Ecuadorable (Ecuadorian American)
8. La Guitarra (Puerto Rican – South)
9. Nuyorican (Puerto Rican – Northeast)
10. Cinnamon Swirl (Dominican American – Florida)
11. Beauty Call (Dominican American – Northeast)
12. Perusian (Peruvian American)
13. Pupusa (Salvadoran American)
14. Hotemalan (Guatemalan American)

As you'll see, America's Latinas aren't perfect — nobody is — but they're getting the guy now more than ever because they offer an appealing alternative to emasculation by hostile, manly American women. This trend is likely to intensify as language barriers dissipate *unless* American women stop taking dating and relationship advice from militant feminists and get back in the game. There's a lot of catching up to do.

Finally, before you delve into the profiles, please review this key to the behavioral trait chart and promiscuity zipper included in each one:

- **Friendliness** (with one smiley face as least friendly and five as most): Friendliness refers to how approachable and gregarious she is, how much she laughs and smiles, and how quickly she warms to strangers.

- **Neuroticism** (with one bloody cleaver as least neurotic and five as most): Neuroticism refers to how stressed out, anxious, or potentially psychotic she is or appears to be.

- **Nesting** (with one bird's nest as least interested in marriage and kids, and five as most): Nesting refers to how determined and likely she is to get married young, have kids, and settle down—but also reflects the priority that she tends to place on family, and how often she sacrifices career to be a homemaker or stay-at-home mom.

- **Maintenance** (with one hammer as lowest maintenance and five as highest): Maintenance refers to how much love, attention, or support she needs to feel satisfied in a relationship.

- **Superficiality** (with one bag of money as least superficial and five as most): Superficiality refers to how many purely superficial considerations (e.g., money, looks, or ethnicity) play into mate selection and serve as powerful chica magnets.

- **Promiscuity** (with one, zipped up, as least promiscuous and ten, unzipped, as most): Promiscuity refers to how likely she is to sleep around and have casual sex while single.

That's all I have to say about that.

Now, let's go people watching. Oops, I meant *chicaspotting*.

PARTS OF A CHICA

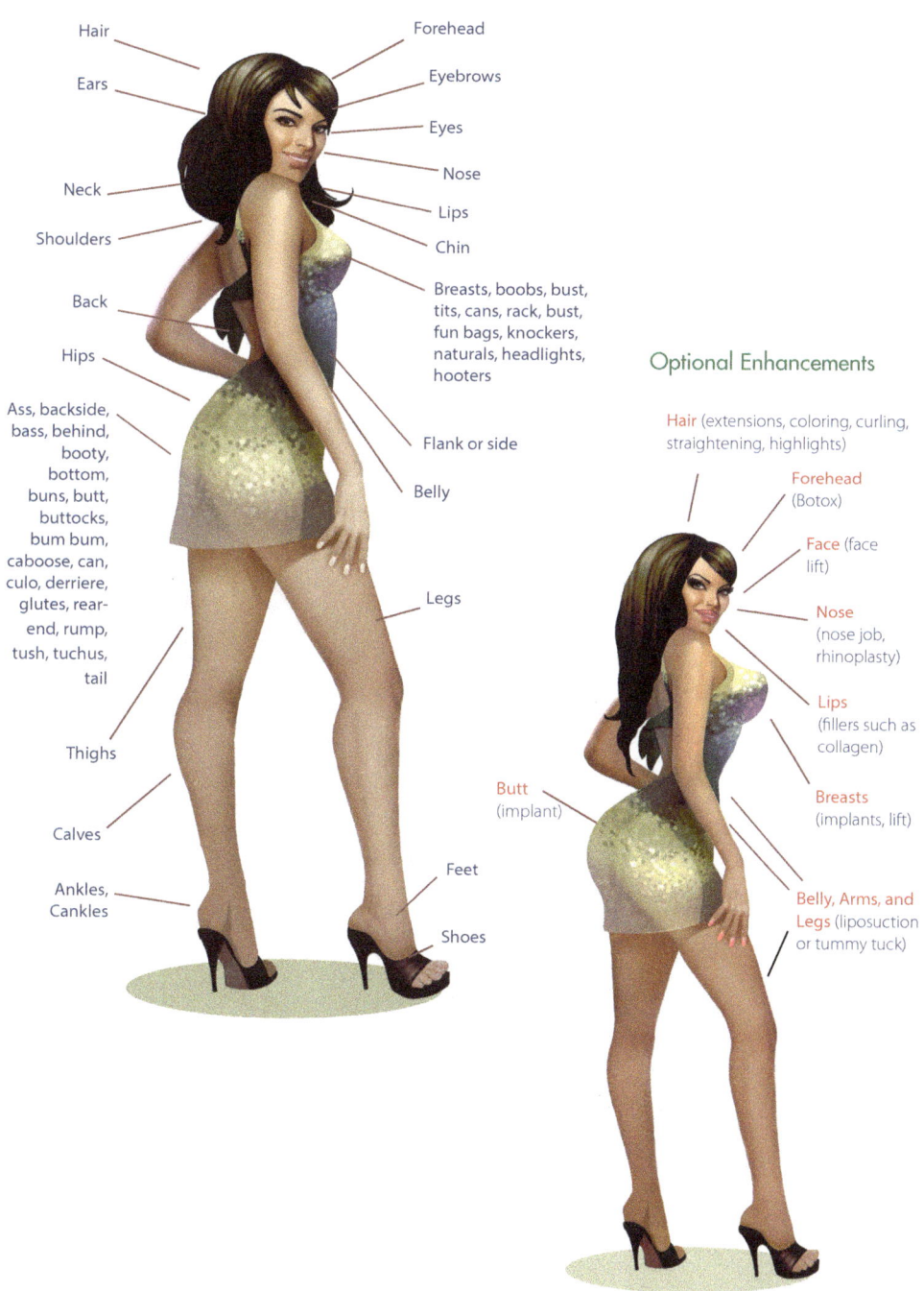

Hair
Ears
Neck
Shoulders
Back
Hips
Ass, backside, bass, behind, booty, bottom, buns, butt, buttocks, bum bum, caboose, can, culo, derriere, glutes, rear-end, rump, tush, tuchus, tail
Thighs
Calves
Ankles, Cankles

Forehead
Eyebrows
Eyes
Nose
Lips
Chin
Breasts, boobs, bust, tits, cans, rack, bust, fun bags, knockers, naturals, headlights, hooters
Flank or side
Belly
Legs
Feet
Shoes

Optional Enhancements

Hair (extensions, coloring, curling, straightening, highlights)
Forehead (Botox)
Face (face lift)
Nose (nose job, rhinoplasty)
Lips (fillers such as collagen)
Breasts (implants, lift)
Butt (implant)
Belly, Arms, and Legs (liposuction or tummy tuck)

WHY LATINAS GET THE GUY • 35

TACO BELLE™
(Mexican American)

APPEARANCE: This chica — not to be confused with Taco Bell® fast food — is recognizable by her dusky complexion with heavy makeup, brown hair, brown eyes, and facial features that reveal Native American ancestry. Normally curvy and petite or medium-sized, with large or medium-sized breasts and a wide butt that's flat at the top and round at the bottom. Often out of shape because exercise is less emphasized in Mexican culture, but wears very tight jeans and shirts with a bare midriff to show off her figure anyway. Rarely wears unflattering gym clothes in public or gets tattoos, which are still considered trashy in Mexico.

NOTABLES

Eva Longoria, Thalia, Elsa Benitez, Erica Erana, Mia St. John, Claudia Salinas, Erika Medina, Cindy Martinez, Pennelope Jimenez, and Cierra Ramirez.

TO HAVE AND TO HOLD

Sara Ramirez, a curvy, size 14 (at best) Taco Belle actress known for her role on the *Grey's Anatomy* TV show, summed up one of the benefits of her extra pounds this way: "I know my boyfriend loves to have something to hold on to. There are a lot of men out there who do." That's true, but stunning Eva Longoria shows how hot a Taco Belle can be if she exercises regularly.

BEHAVIOR: Warm and cuddly as a teddy bear but (somewhat) shy around strangers, especially gringos. Values Mexican culture, with its focus on family, religion (mainly Catholic), love, and tradition. Normally hardworking but not particularly ambitious or well-educated because she doesn't want career to interfere with family. This generation is far more driven and independent, however. Frequently works in a (blue-collar) service industry or as a skilled artisan. Loves dancing, music, food, and family gatherings.

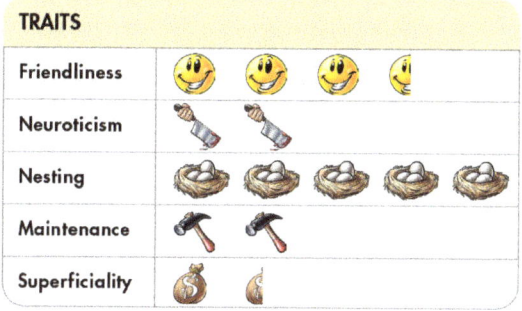

SONG: Generally soft-spoken but much louder in her comfort zone with friends and family. Uses exaggerated tones and gestures to convey passion and a sense of drama, as you can plainly see on any Mexican soap opera. Often prefers to speak Spanish as much as possible.

DON'T BE SO SARCASTIC

Sarcasm is considered disrespectful in Mexican culture and doesn't translate well into Spanish.

MATING: Highly feminine but demands respect. Often (somewhat) dependent on her man. Exceptionally sentimental, attentive, and nurturing but melodramatic and smothering at times. Seductive and sensual but reluctant to have sex before a level of trust has been established, unless she's relatively young and rebellious. Occasionally sleeps with white guys sooner than usual because they're perceived as less judgmental than Mexican men, and her Catholic sense of shame has faded considerably in recent years. Known to wait three dates to two months (or more) before closing the deal.

MAGNETS: Attracted to Latin (primarily Mexican) and white gentlemen who are respectful, family-oriented, and capable of making her feel safe and secure. Seldom a gold digger but expects to be supported financially and emotionally. Often drawn to significantly older men because age isn't a big deal in Mexican culture and is associated with many positive qualities. Guys who speak Spanish or show a genuine interest in her culture also have a big edge. Rarely attracted to "bad boys" unless she's lower-class and/or doesn't identify with Mexican culture much anymore.

BEING OLDER CAN WORK IN A GUY'S FAVOR

Most American women aren't interested in considerably older men unless they're wealthy and, ahem, generous. Not so the Taco Belle. She's often physically attracted to much older men for cultural reasons having little or nothing to do with money.

HABITAT: Mexican party or nightclub; soccer game; Catholic Church; Latin music concert.

LOCATION: Abundant in Texas, especially San Elizario, Tornillo, Lopezville, Progreso, Cameron Park, Presidio, Alton, Hidalgo, Cactus, Penitas, Palmview, Roma, Fort Hancock, Heidelberg, San Juan, and La Joya; California, especially Calexico, Coachella, Huron, Parlier, Lost Hills, Mecca, East Los Angeles, and San Joaquin; and Arizona, especially Somerton and Nogales. Abundant to some what common in parts of Washington, New Mexico, Nevada, Idaho, Illinois, Florida, Utah, and Colorado.

MIGRATION: Migratory.

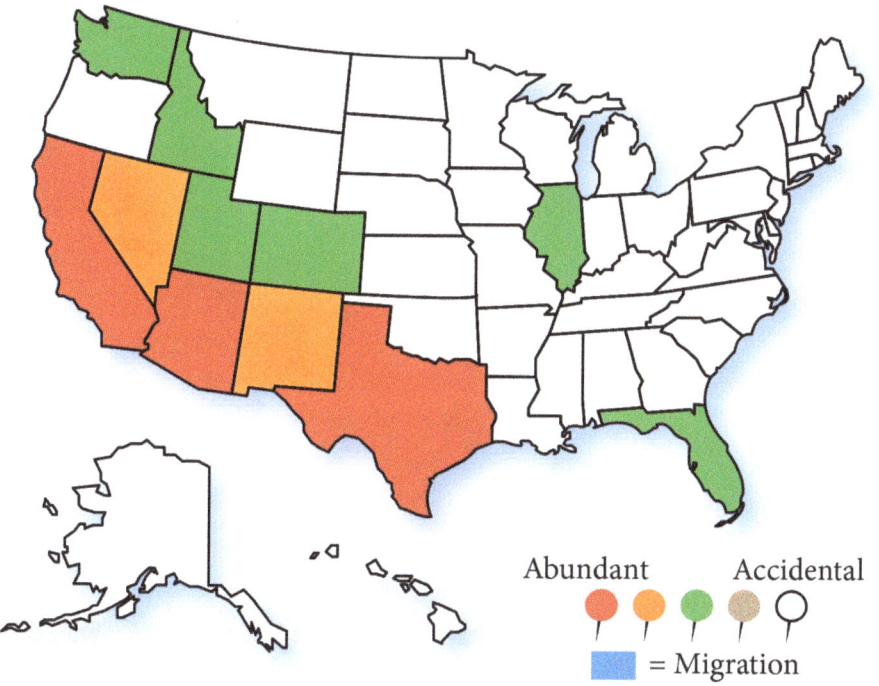

WHY LATINAS GET THE GUY • 39

BUMBSHELL™
(Brazilian American)

40 • WHY LATINAS GET THE GUY

APPEARANCE: Ask this happy-go-lucky chica about her best feature and chances are she'll turn around and show you her big, cheeky bum bum. Other field marks include strong, sexy legs; a small waist; naturally small breasts (but boob jobs are increasingly common); a lean, athletic frame; twinkling brown eyes; full lips; and a warm smile. Often a curly or wavy-haired brunette with optional highlights. Complexion varies from golden to dark brown. Dresses to be sexy and loves to wear a skimpy Brazilian bikini with optional anklet.

NOTABLES

Adriana Lima, Camila Alves-McConaughey, Alessandra Ambrosia, Isabeli Fontana, Gisele Bundchen, Alice Braga, Gleicy Santos, and Morena Baccarin.

BEHAVIOR: Exceptionally happy, positive, sociable, and non-confrontational. Rarely loses her sense of humor or takes life too seriously. Spontaneous and adventurous but seldom punctual. Social life revolves around family and friends, not work. Often religious (Roman Catholic and Protestant) and interested in astrology, psychic readings, or other mystic pursuits.

TRAITS					
Friendliness	😃	😃	😃	😃	😃
Neuroticism	🔪	🔪			
Nesting	🥚	🥚	🥚	🥚	
Maintenance	🔨	🔨	🔨	🔨	
Superficiality	💰	💰	💰		

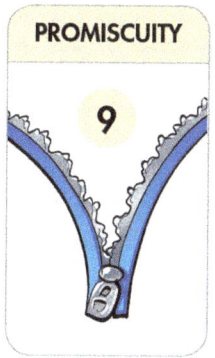

PROMISCUITY: 9

SONG: Enjoys small talk, laughter, and affection as means of communication. Brazilian Portuguese, not Spanish, is her native tongue. Normally doesn't even like the sound of Spanish. Known to baffle gringos because "Yes" (Sim) means anything from "Yes" to "Perhaps" to "No;" "Perhaps" (Talvez) means "No;" "No" (Não) means "Absolutely never. Not in a million years. This is the craziest thing I've ever been asked;" "A hug! A kiss!" (Um abraço! Um beijo!) means "Take care. Bye;" "Let's see" (Vamos ver) means "Not a chance. Please drop it;" and "I'll be there in ten minutes" (Vou chegar em dez minutinhos) means "Sometime in the next half-hour I'll get up off the sofa and start looking for my keys."

MATING: Arguably the most promiscuous of America's Latinas, despite her Christian faith. Loves foreplay, especially kissing. Always fully waxed and ready for action. Highly flirtatious, sensual, and sexually uninhibited but often scandalous and fickle. Typically expects a guy to assume a portion of her extended family's financial obligations in Brazil if the relationship gets serious. Known to wait one to four dates (more or less) before closing the deal.

A KISS IS JUST A KISS

Don't be surprised if the Bumbshell kisses you lustfully in one moment and someone else the same way in the next. She loves to kiss but makes a clear distinction between kissing (which commonly happens fast) and everything else (which normally requires an investment of some time and energy). She may also lie (to spare your feelings), cheat (to indulge her own), or keep ex-boyfriends around (just in case).

MAGNETS: Attracted to men who are successful, generous (with their money, time, and love), family-oriented, and patient when she acts in ways they don't understand. The hotter she is, the more likely she is to be attracted only to rich guys. Tends to assume that white men have money, but may also assume that they're relatively boring (by Brazilian standards), anal-retentive, and uncoordinated (on the dance floor).

UP CLOSE AND PERSONAL

Unlike most American women, the Bumbshell doesn't require much personal space to feel comfortable and is easily approachable. In fact, guys who maintain a safe, respectful, Anglo-Saxon distance risk blowing it when she incorrectly assumes that they're uninterested or gay. She also tends to think that the American accent is sexy, especially when spoken softly into her ear. So move in, fellas. And stay close. A kiss - or more - may await you.

HABITAT: Beach; pool; boat/yacht; beauty/nail salon; gym; health food store; mall; Catholic church; (Brazilian) restaurant; concert; art exhibit; popular lounge or nightclub (with dancing); cool sports bar; private party (with friends).

LOCATION: Somewhat common to casual in New Jersey (especially East Newark, Harrison, Long Branch, and Kearny); south Florida (especially North Bay Village, Bay Harbor Islands, Miamii Beach, North Miami Beach, Surfside, Key Biscayne, Aventura, Doral, Deerfield Beach, Pompano Beach, Oakland Park, and Lighthouse Point); Massachusetts (especially Framingham, Vineyard Haven, Marlborough, and Everett); Danbury, CT; Los Angeles County (especially Redondo Beach and Venice Boulevard in West LA); and "Little Brazil" in NYC.

MIGRATION: Migratory.

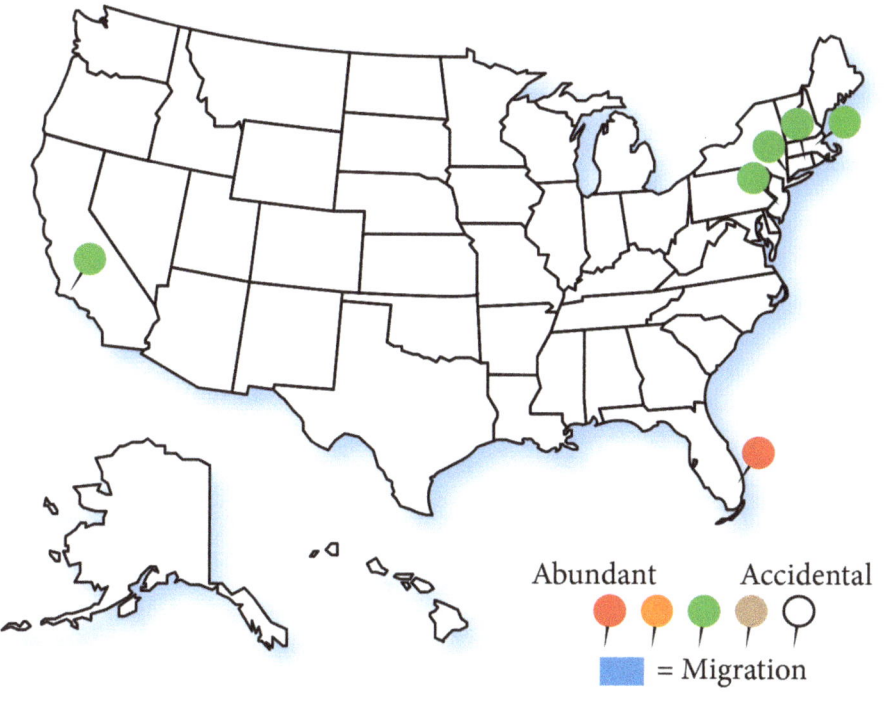

WHY LATINAS GET THE GUY • 43

EURO-MINA™
(Argentine American)

APPEARANCE: The Euro-Mina tends to look more Italian or Spanish than Latin and dresses with a French flair for fashion. (About 90% of Argentines are immigrants from Italy and Spain and their descendants.) Almost always slender — Argentina has one of the highest rates of anorexia — with a petite frame and small bone structure, but still somewhat shapely, although not in a Barbie doll way. Less likely to supersize a boob job or wear heavy makeup than other Latin American chicas. Often has straight, dark hair (although a minority are naturally or artificially blond), fair to light brown skin, and striking (dark) eyes.

NOTABLES

Marianela Pereyra, Yamila Díaz-Rahi (aka Yamila Diaz), Luján Fernández, Inés Rivero, Luciana Scarabello, Inés Rivero, and Julie Gonzalo.

BEHAVIOR: Warm and friendly around people she likes but occasionally snobbish, condescending, and dismissive to others, especially blacks, Asians, and non-Argentines. Family-oriented, emotional, and passionate but in more of a Southern European than Latin way. Outgoing, proud, and confident but realistic and aware of her own shortcomings. Relatively well-educated and industrious. Loves dancing (especially the tango), music, and the outdoors. Predominantly Roman Catholic but, like many Europeans, rarely goes to church.

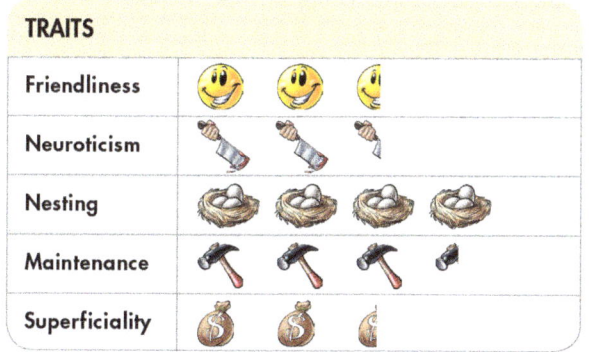

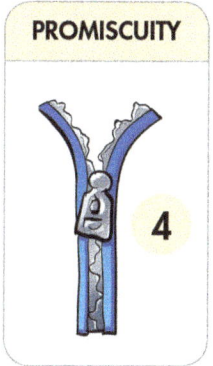

SONG: Expresses her opinions in a direct and open way. Says and does whatever it takes to get her point across. Doesn't hesitate to criticize others, raise her voice, curse, or point out how others (without her Southern European ancestry) are less cultured.

NO PATIENCE FOR POLITICAL CORRECTNESS

The Euro-Mina has something to say, a right to say it, and no patience for political correctness. If you can't handle it, it's your problem, not hers.

MATING: Enjoys little dating games and playing hard to get, unlike many Latin American chicas. Amorous but seldom sleeps with a guy on the first date and isn't particularly interested in casual sex. Frequently a bit demanding, possessive, jealous, and territorial, however. Moody or whiny too at times. Known to wait three weeks to two months before closing the deal.

KEEP HER GUESSING

The Euro-Mina needs a challenge and doesn't mind taking on a player or bad boy. She can handle whoever comes her way in stride. Smart men pursue her aggressively but inject a little uncertainty about their level of interest.

MAGNETS: Traditionally attracted to real men ("machistas") with strong personalities who are self-assured, charismatic, and charming, but increasingly tired of the extreme, stereotypical version. Normally goes for white or Latin guys but occasionally dates other types with lots of personality, intelligence, and/or money.

NO BETA MALES

Always approach the Euro-Mina self-assuredly. She may even overlook the fact that you're not particularly good-looking if you don't seem intimidated. Fearlessness — real or feigned — is sexy.

HABITAT: City restaurant; café; shopping mall; polo match; park; lounge or nightclub (with dancing); party; beach.

LOCATION: Somewhat common in Miami Beach, Sunny Isles Beach, Plantation Mobile Home Park, Bay Harbor Islands, North Bay Village, Key Biscayne, Surfside, Lauderdale-by-the-Sea, The Crossings, Ojus, Doral, and Aventura, FL; Deer Park, Acton, and East Richmond Heights, CA; Harbor Hills, Islandia, and Thomaston, NY; Lebanon, IL; and Mayland-Pleasant Hill, TN. Casual to accidental in other metropolitan areas of South Florida; New York City; Houston and Dallas, TX; California, Illinois, New York, New Jersey, Connecticut, and Western Pennsylvania.

MIGRATION: Migratory.

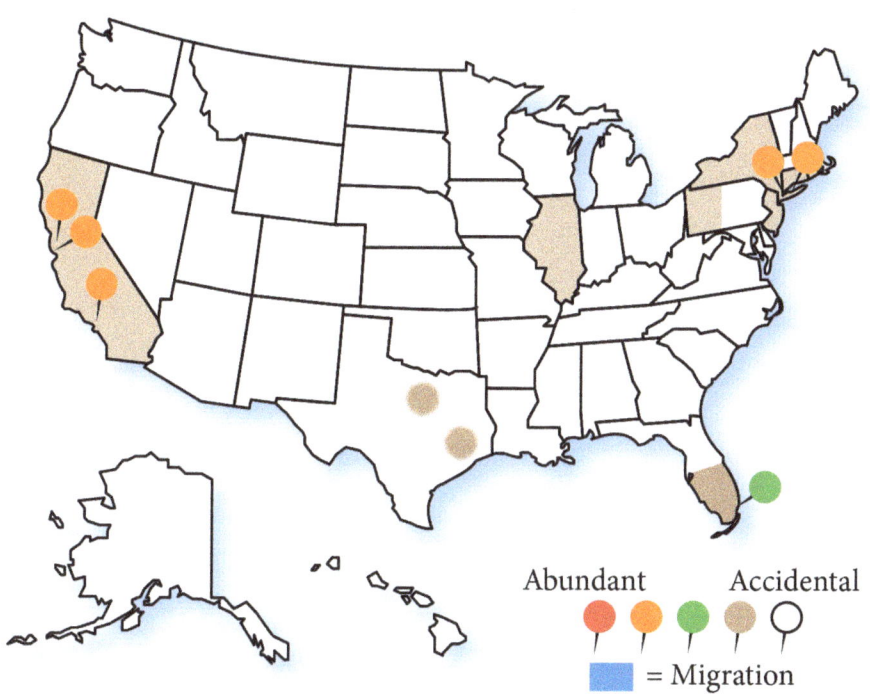

WHY LATINAS GET THE GUY • 47

SYMMETRICAL FORCE
(Colombian American)

APPEARANCE: Look for delicate, symmetrical features on a round, cute-as-a-button face; a big smile; long, dark brown or black hair that's silky smooth and straight or slightly wavy; wide-set brown eyes (often with a slight slant or bronze circles underneath); and soft bronzed or brown skin. Normally petite, finely-toned, and symmetrically shaped. Bust size varies, but breast implants are practically a rite of passage and she likes 'em **BIG**. Tends to seek aesthetic perfection through a nose job, liposuction, butt implants, or collagen injections. Impeccably well groomed, made-up, and maintained. Over-accessorizes with big belts, earrings, and the whole nine yards. Unafraid to wear white pants.

NOTABLES

Sophia Vergara, Manuela Arbeláez (*The Price is Right*), Monica Fonseca, Maria Checa, Karen Carreno, Lina Maya, Evelin Santos, Cindy Luna, Alba Galindo, and Ximena Duque.

BEHAVIOR: Exceptionally charming and gregarious but worldly, shrewd, and mysterious. Family-oriented, proud, and somewhat religious (mainly Roman Catholic) but intense, materialistic, and deeply cynical, especially about men. Surprisingly bright and entrepreneurial, but more likely to pursue a shortcut to success and the easiest way to get what she wants. Often places a higher priority on parties and dating than working or studying. Dances merengue, vallenato, cumbia, or salsa beautifully without any music. Easily annoyed if mistaken for another Latin American species, especially the *Taco Belle*.

TRAITS					
Friendliness	😀	😀	😀	😀	😀
Neuroticism	🔨	🔨	🔨	🔨	
Nesting	🪺	🪺	🪺	🪺	
Maintenance	🔨	🔨	🔨	🔨	🔨
Superficiality	💰	💰	💰	💰	💰

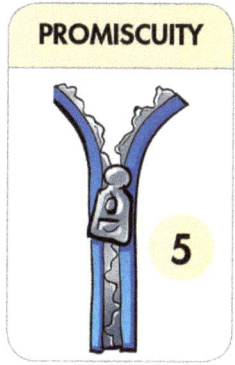

PROMISCUITY 5

WATCH YOUR BACK

Many Latinas secretly fear the Symmetrical Force because they know what a smooth and cunning operator lies beneath the sugary-sweet demeanor. They don't buy the whole nice-girl routine. Some of this anxiety comes from jealousy and possessiveness, but most comes from experience. So watch your back while you're watching hers.

SONG: Chatty and demonstrative, especially in singsong Spanish. Loves to laugh but loud and excitable at times. Often refers to all whites as "gringos" and all Asians as "Chinese." Common expressions include "Regalamelo." (Give it to me as a gift.)

MATING: Tries to be loyal but assumes that men will cheat from day one and occasionally beats them to the punch. Exceptional beauty coupled with an intense desire for comfort and security often translate into at least some measure of (direct or indirect) gold digging, game-playing, or visa-hunting. Sensual and attentive but exhausting at times. Known to wait two weeks to two months before closing the deal (but expedites the process for rich guys).

MAGNETS: Attracted mainly to Latin, white, or Middle Eastern guys who are financially secure (because men are providers in her culture), generous (with their money), family-oriented, and convivial. It also helps to be well-mannered, clean — she's meticulous about cleanliness and odors — and Catholic.

GIFTS AND CALLS

Arguably the most materialistic of America's Latinas, the Symmetrical Force isn't embarrassed or ashamed about some subtle gold digging, but thoughtful little gifts (e.g., books or flowers) go a long way for interested suitors. She also expects a guy to call the day after a kiss and will hold it against him forever if he doesn't. Sending a text message usually won't suffice.

HABITAT: Beauty salon; gym; beach; mall; trendy boutique; restaurant or bar; dance club; (exclusive) party; boat; church; (Latin music) concert; sporting event; red-carpet affair.

LOCATION: Common to somewhat common in New Jersey (especially Victory Gardens, Dover, Morristown, Englewood, West New York, and North Bergen); south Florida, with high concentrations in Miami (especially the booming Brickell financial district) and its suburbs (especially Doral, Kendall, and Hialeah), Country Club, Virginia Gardens, Key Biscayne, Kendale Lakes, Weston, and Sunny Isles Beach; Central Falls, RI; and parts of New York City (especially Queens, Montauk, Jackson Heights, and East Hampton North.

MIGRATION: Migratory.

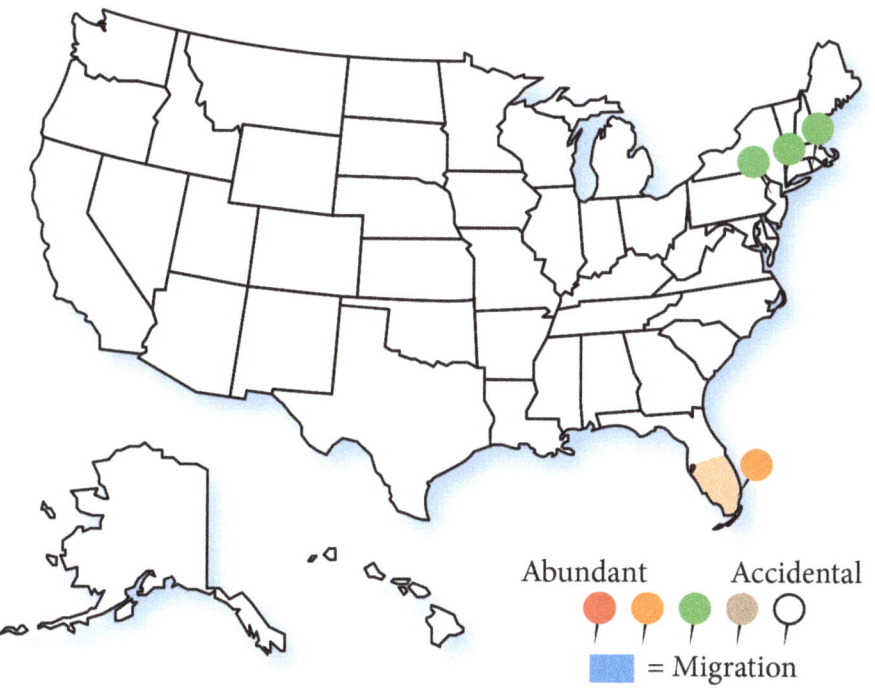

WHY LATINAS GET THE GUY • 51

ECUADORABLE™
(Ecuadorian American)

APPEARANCE: This diamond in the rough is a mix of Spanish, Indian, and/or African ancestry. She tends to be unusually skinny for a Latina — except for the even thinner and lighter-skinned *Euro-Mina* from Argentina — but manages to maintain her curves and shapely figure anyway. Other field marks include delicate facial features (including a tiny nose) on a small face, and straight, black (or colored) hair. Almost always tanned, well-groomed, stylishly dressed, and petite to medium height. Eye color varies.

BEHAVIOR: Tends to be outgoing, energetic, and happy-go-lucky but quite stubborn and aloof. Courteous, religious (Catholic), and "old-school" traditional in many ways but gets lost in her own world once in a while. Often bright, independent, and entrepreneurial without losing focus on the family. Loves to dance (merengue and salsa), cook, travel, and meet people of different ethnicities and cultures.

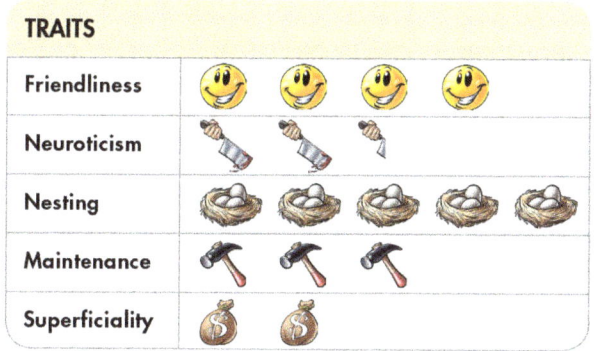
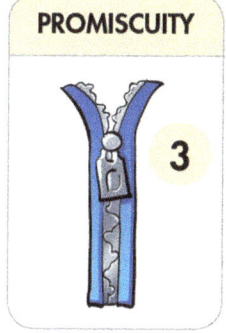

SONG: Outspoken, talkative, hard-headed (in fights), and slow to admit when she's wrong. Loud at times.

GROUND RULES

A guy who's looking for a strictly casual (sexual) relationship with an Ecuadorable will be fine as long as he tells the truth up front. He probably won't get laid, but she won't hold it against him either.

MATING: Family-oriented but tends to call the shots in hers, one way or another. Horny and sexually adventurous but not easily taken to bed. (Well worth the wait, however). Demands attention, commitment, and plenty of sex in a relationship but wants her man to be just as satisfied. Rarely hot-tempered unless she discovers that you're a liar or a fraud, in which case you should run for the hills. Reliably loving, faithful, and loyal, but don't push her buttons. Known to wait one or two months before closing the deal.

MAGNETS: Attracted to men with similar views about family and career who take the lead, make her feel protected, and express a sincere interest in settling down. Usually dates Latin, white or Middle Eastern guys.

HABITAT: Beach; pool; dance club; (karaoke) bar; café or lounge; (business) networking event; family gathering; private party with close friends.

LOCATION: Somewhat common to casual in New York, especially Sleepy Hollow, Montauk, Patchogue, Ossining, Port Chester, Springs, Peekskill, East Hampton, and New York City (mainly Jackson Heights, Brooklyn, and the Bronx); New Jersey, especially East Newark, Hightstown, Union City, Hackensack, West New York, North Bergen, Harrison, Guttenberg, East Windsor, Dover, Belleville, Jersey City, Union City, and Plainfield; Florida (especially Miami, Orlando, and Fort Lauderdale); and Danbury, Connecticut. Casual in Chicago, IL, Minneapolis, MN, and Los Angeles, CA.

MIGRATION: Migratory.

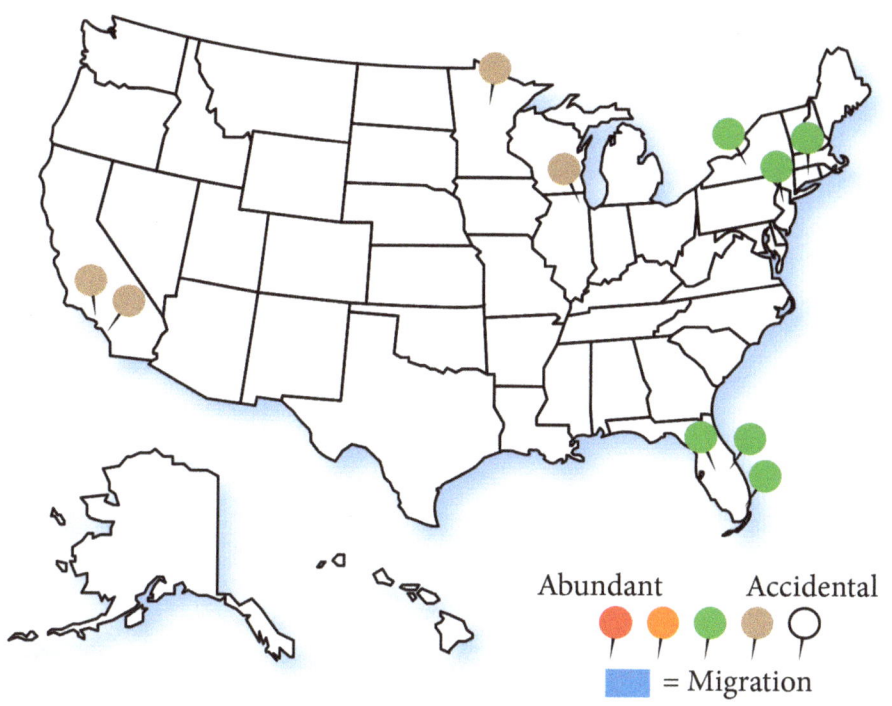

WHY LATINAS GET THE GUY • 55

LA GUITARRA™
(Puerto Rican – South)

APPEARANCE: This dangerously curvy chica, also known as "Mami Boricua" or "Boricua Mami," is recognizable by her guitar-shaped body, with a thick, shapely butt — similar to the leaner version of the Cuban American *Transformer* and a little thicker than a Brazilian American *Bumbshell* — tiny waist, and naturally small to medium-sized breasts. Often gets a boob job to balance things out. Normally petite to medium-height with distinctively golden brown skin derived from a mixture of Spanish and African ancestry, also known as "mancha de platano" (plantain-banana stain), sexy brown eyes, and long, dark brown hair. Commonly wears sexy, colorfully stylish clothing and accessories.

NOTABLES

Roselyn Sánchez, Zuleyka Rivera, Victoria Justice (1/2 white), Joyce Giraud, Jaslene Gonzalez, and Gina Rodriquez (possibly *Nuyorican* or *La Guitarra/Nuyorican*).

SHE'S NO VISA-HUNTER

Unlike many Latinas in the United States these days, La Guitarra doesn't need to marry to get a green card. She's already a U.S. citizen.

BEHAVIOR: Devoted to family and faith (mainly Catholic). Proud to be Puerto Rican but with something to prove in the USA. Well-assimilated with other Latinos in Miami, Orlando, and other US cities outside the Northeast. Normally affable, gregarious, and bright but (somewhat) ostentatious. Usually smart, responsible, and sympathetic. Rarely associates with the *Nuyorican* (her Puerto Rican counterpart in New York and other parts of the Northeast) because of vast cultural differences between them. Loves to cook and dances remarkably well.

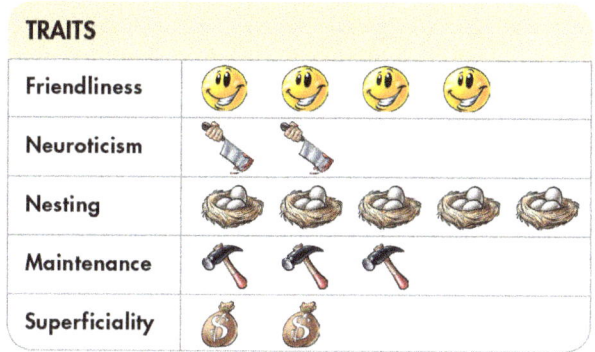

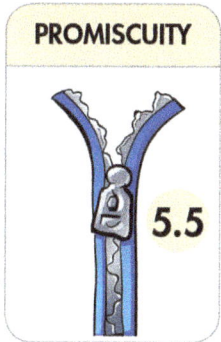

SONG: Talks quickly, laughs frequently, and loves to gesture with her hands. Multi-lingual but often prefers Spanish to English.

MATING: Feels pressure to remain a virgin or at least sustain the illusion until she ties the knot, which usually happens before she turns 25. Stops working after marriage to be a full-time housewife because family is her highest priority. Nurturing, considerate, and passionate but temperamental, jealous, and extremely territorial. Generally loyal but won't tolerate bad behavior indefinitely. Known to wait three weeks to two months before closing the deal.

READY OR NOT

Once a committed relationship has been established, La Guitarra will want sex as much or more than her man does, no matter how hot she is. And not just in bed at night. She'll come at him in the shower, the kitchen, the closet, the garage, and just about anywhere else. He should be ready to go at all times.

MAGNETS: Attracted mainly to Latin guys but occasionally dates white and Middle Eastern ones with similar values and behavioral tendencies. Seldom branches out from there.

HABITAT: Nail salon; beach; dance club; restaurant or bar; Catholic Church; private party with close friends and family; airport (especially MIA).

LOCATION: Common to somewhat common in Florida, especially Miami Gardens and other parts of Miami-Dade County, Yeehaw Junction, Poinciana, Azalea Park, Kissimmee, Interlachen, Union Park, and Buenaventura Lakes. Somewhat common in Orlando and Tampa, FL. Casual to accidental in other parts of the country, especially Chicago, Philadelphia, Cleveland, and parts of NC, VA, WI, MD, MA, and NJ.

MIGRATION: Migratory (mostly between the continental US and Puerto Rico).

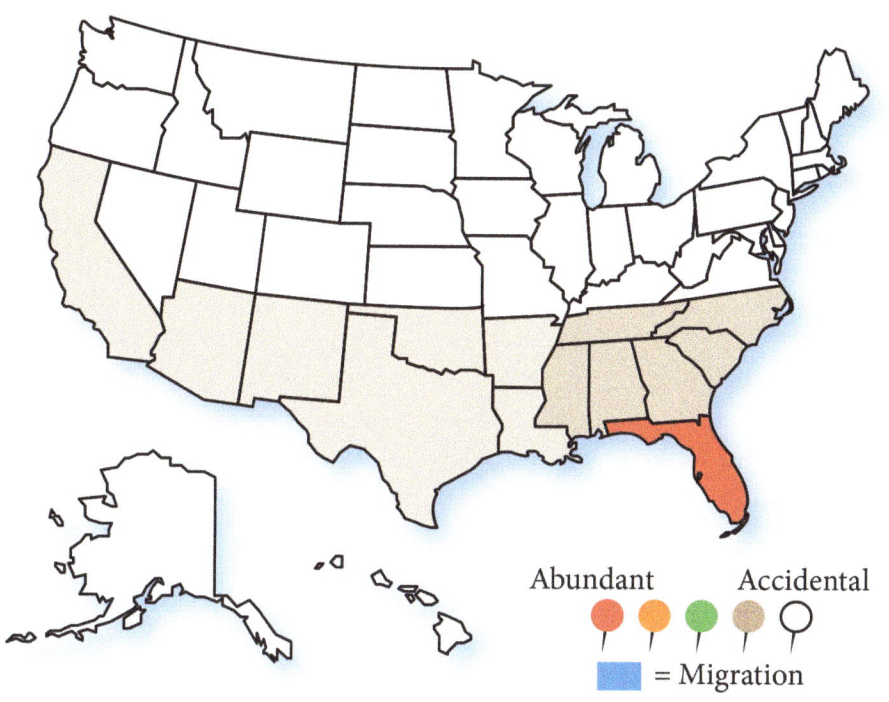

NUYORICAN
(Puerto Rican – Northeast)

APPEARANCE: The Nuyorican [noo-yorree-kan], also known as the "Ledge" or the "Shelf," tends to have an urban or ghetto-urban style due to extensive intermingling of Latin and black cultures in the region, but she glams it up at times. Look for a big, protruding butt, with naturally small to medium-sized breasts, golden brown skin, a prominent forehead, beautiful brown eyes, and long, dark brown hair. Often petite to medium-height. Breast implants are not the norm but increasingly common.

TWO POTATOES ON STICKS

Jennifer Lopez is America's most famous Nuyorican. She put it this way: "As a Latin woman in the United States, you're taught that you should be skinnier, that you shouldn't have such a big butt. You feel self-conscious. I did. I was really thin, but I had a booty on me that you would not believe, like two potatoes on sticks." There was, however, a fringe benefit: "I could serve coffee using my rear as a ledge."

NOTABLES

Rosario Dawson, Rosie Perez, Adrienne Bailon (1/2 *Ecuadorable*), LaLa Anthony, Jennifer Lopez, Talisa Soto, and Gina Rodriquez (possibly *La Guitarra* or *La Guitarra/Nuyorican*).

BEHAVIOR: Family-oriented and spirited but not particularly friendly to strangers and occasionally somewhat aggressive. Too often relatively uneducated and poor — with a poverty rate similar to the African-American *Bronx Tail* — but animated and passionate about life. Usually loves urban and Latin music (including lots of reggaeton), watching the "novelas," dancing, and singing.

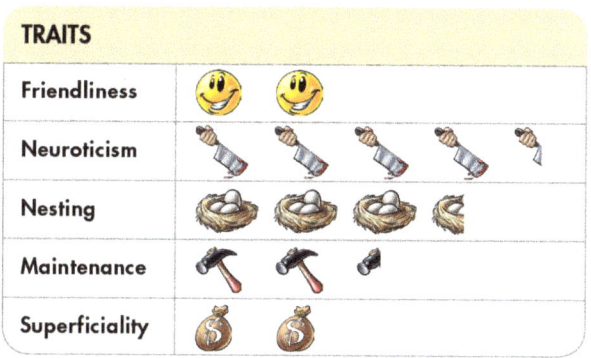

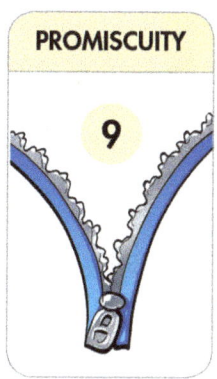

DUAL IDENTITY

The Nuyorican has a dual identity (crisis) because she shares cultural traits with fully assimilated American blacks in the Northeast that differ greatly from the *La Guitarra* in South Florida and Puerto Rico.

SONG: Talks quickly and loudly. Tends to curse, use urban slang, say "culo" (ass) and "Que carajo!" (What the f*ck!), mangle grammar, and gesture dramatically. Often refers to her man affectionately as "papi" (daddy) or "chulo" (cutie) unless she's upset with him, in which case he's a "pendejo" (dumbass) or "sangano" (idiot). Frequently speaks English (or Spanglish) rather than Spanish but conversant in both languages.

MATING: Fickle, sexy, and promiscuous while single, but extremely territorial in any exclusive relationship. Tends to have a non-traditional family structure and stay single longer than most other Latin-American species. If she has a child out of wedlock — as often happens — she'll go after the biological father for child support until she gets it or they repo his ride. Known to wait one night to two weeks before closing the deal.

MAGNETS: Attracted mainly to Latin and black guys, especially bad boys and players. Occasionally dates other types with a compatibly urban lifestyle and worldview.

HABITAT: Dominican hair salon; party; concert; local (urban) club, restaurant, or shop; National Puerto Rican Day Parade in New York City.

LOCATION: Abundant to common in New York, especially New York City, with the largest Puerto Rican community outside Puerto Rico, and the Bronx; New Jersey, especially Camden, Perth Amboy, Newark, and Vineland; Pennsylvania, especially Lancaster, Reading, Allentown, and (North) Philadelphia; Massachusetts, especially Holyoke, Springfield, and Lawrence; Connecticut, especially Hartford, Bridgeport, and New Britain; and parts of (central and northern) Florida, especially Orlando; Cleveland-Lorain- Elyria, Ohio; and Chicago, Illinois.

MIGRATION: Somewhat migratory.

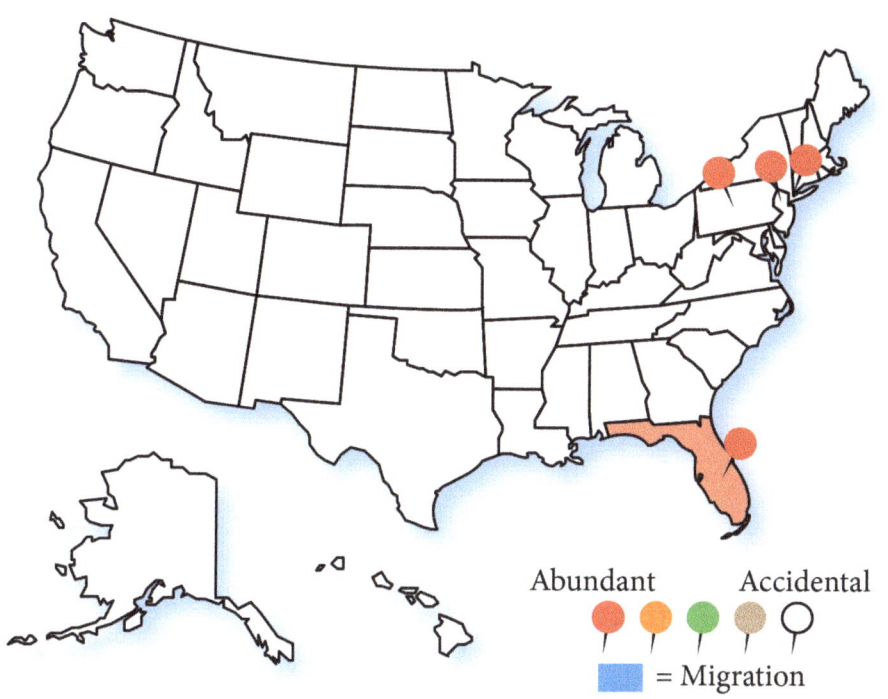

TRIFECTA™
(Venezuelan American)

APPEARANCE: Also known as "Miss Venezuela" or "La Perfecta," this high-stakes chica is always beauty-pageant ready, no matter how old she is. Normally medium-height — and slightly taller than the Colombian American *Symmetrical Force* if you're having trouble telling the difference — with a lean, curvy body; olive or bronzed skin (with optional freckles, especially on her chest, back, or shoulders); long, dark (or bleached blond) hair; and expressive eyes. Natural breasts tend to be small to medium-sized, but large fake boobs are common. Doesn't hesitate to get a nose job or other cosmetic surgery either. Dresses with style and tries to look sexy at all times without over-accessorizing.

ONLY SMOKING HOT WILL DO

Some of the most beautiful women in the world compete to win the Miss Venezuela beauty pageant every year, and the American version is trying to keep up. This competitive spirit often translates into stunningly good looks.

NOTABLES

Chiquinquirá Delgado, Cristina Abuhazi, Anabelle Blum, Patricia Velásquez, Génesis Rodríguez (1/2 *Transformer*), Majandra Delfino, and Jacqueline Marquez.

SONG: Seductive Spanish accent.

BEHAVIOR: Confident, (brutally) honest, proud, and poised — like the beauty pageant winner she is (in her mind) or wants to be. Engaging and demure but narcissistic, condescending, and callous at times, even if she's not that pretty. Often well-educated, industrious, and ambitious but family-oriented, well-rounded, and religious (mainly Catholic). Emotional with friends and family but somewhat quiet and introverted around strangers.

TRAITS				
Friendliness	😃	😃	😃	😃
Neuroticism	🍾	🍾	🍾	
Nesting	🪺	🪺	🪺	🪺
Maintenance	🔨	🔨	🔨	🔨
Superficiality	💰	💰	💰	

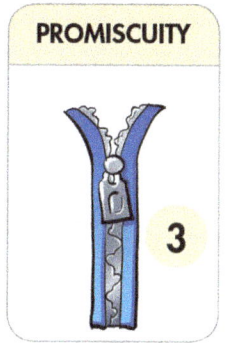

PROMISCUITY 3

NOT JUST ANOTHER REALLY PRETTY FACE

The Trifecta normally isn't content to rely on her good looks to get ahead. She's just as likely to be an engineer, professional, or entrepreneur as a model, actress, or beauty queen.

MATING: Routinely causes an erection lasting more than four hours, but neediness, jealousy, and controlling behavior — a real "Trifecta" of drama — occasionally spoil the mood. (The Venezuelan slang word for a very jealous or ill-tempered woman is "Cuaima.") If a guy is fortunate enough to get the Trifecta into bed and make all the right moves, she'll return the favor and more. Known to wait one or two months before closing the deal.

MAGNETS: Attracted to gentlemen who treat her like a princess or (beauty) queen. Often dates Latin or white men who are respectful, protective, and capable of settling down. Expects men to treat waiters, housekeepers, and others with dignity and respect too, especially in her presence. Charming and charismatic risk-takers also have an edge, especially if the risks pay off in financial success.

ADD SOME SALT

If you're white, the Trifecta is likely to assume that you're "una papa sin sal" (a potato without salt) — in other words, boring. Prove her wrong by taking risks and having some fun. Stand out from the other potatoes.

HABITAT: Beauty salon; beauty pageant or competition; modeling or casting agency; gym; Catholic church; mall; university; office building; beach; yacht or nice boat.

LOCATION: Common to somewhat common in South Florida, especially in the suburbs of Doral, Weston, Fontainebleau, The Hammocks, Key Biscayne, North Bay Village, Sunny Isles Beach, and Miami Beach. Casual in New York City and Los Angeles.

MIGRATION: Migratory.

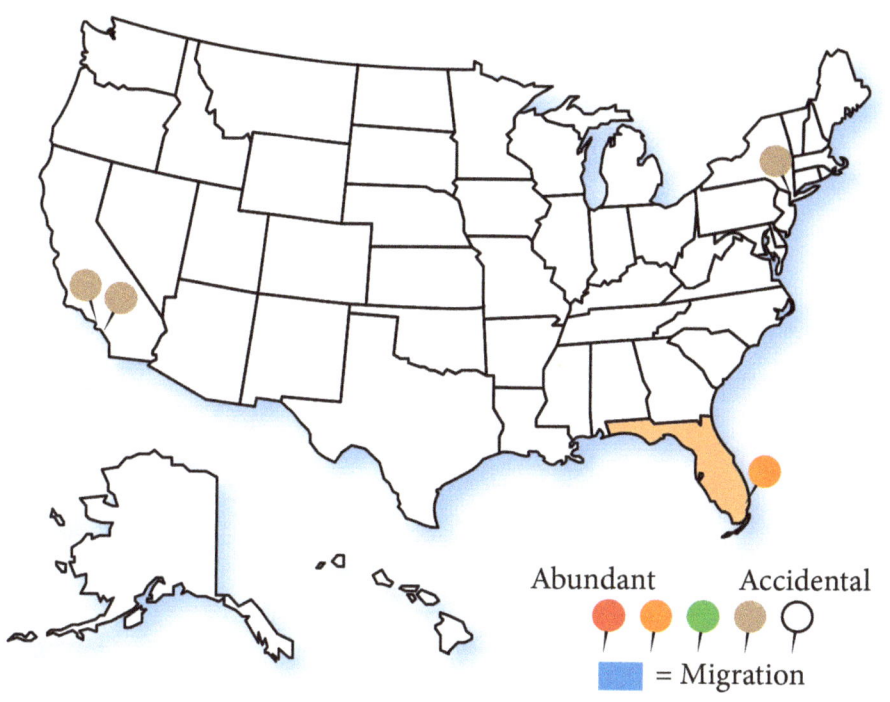

Abundant Accidental

= Migration

TRANSFORMER™
(Cuban American)

68 • WHY LATINAS GET THE GUY

APPEARANCE: This fiery Latina is recognizable by her "thick" hips and thighs, big shapely butt, small waist, and short upper body. She also tends to have brown or dyed blond hair, a round face, and brown, oval-shaped eyes. Skin tone ranges from fair to dark brown depending on her mix of Spanish and African ancestry. As comfortable in a business suit as a bikini. Dresses to look sexy and draw attention to her best assets, even if she's fat, because she thinks she's hot either way.

WATCH THE KIDS AND CALS

If her breasts are large enough to match her hips and butt, the Transformer can be a Latin Jessica Rabbit, but too much Cuban food or too many kids and she'll transform into Kirstie Alley right before your eyes.

NOTABLES

Ana Karla Suarez, Eva Mendes, María Canals Barrera, Josie Loren, Génesis Rodríguez (1/2 *Trifecta*), Bella Thorne, Natalie Martinez, Christina Milian, and Daisy Fuentes.

BEHAVIOR: Normally extroverted, friendly, and fun-loving, but headstrong and dominant. Tends to be reasonably well-educated but (overly) contentious and bumptious at times, especially if she's young and lower-class. Family-oriented and religious (mainly Catholic) but savvy, street-smart, and assiduous. Naturally musical.

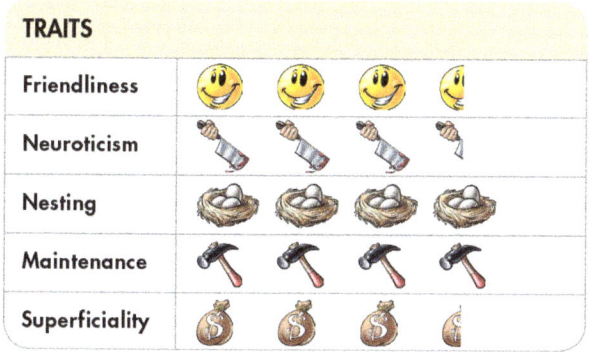
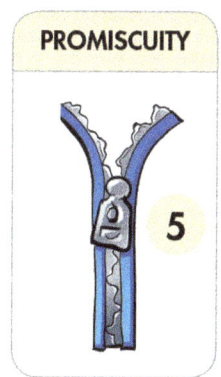

SONG: Outspoken, highly opinionated, and political. Exceptionally loud at times. Gestures frequently with her arms and hands while speaking any language. Speaks Spanish with a thick Cuban accent that even non-Cuban Latinos can't understand at times.

MATING: Even more aggressive than a Cuban guy when she's in an exclusive relationship. Intensely passionate, sensual, and caring but jealous, demanding, and possessive, sometimes exceptionally so. Playful in bed, where sex becomes an outlet for her pent-up feelings of love and lust. Known to wait one month (more or less) before closing the deal.

THE ULTIMATE FIGHTER

This chica stays in charge and gets what she wants from a relationship, no matter what. If she has to fight to get it, so be it. Stand in her way at your own risk.

MAGNETS: Attracted mainly to successful Latin guys, especially muscle-bound Cuban-American ones. Occasionally dates white guys with similar traits and characteristics. Men who can dance also have an edge.

YOU SNOOZE, YOU LOSE

The Transformer expects American men to take the initiative because that's what Cuban guys do, especially the older ones. If a man waits for her to do more than flirt from a distance, she'll assume that he's disinterested, timid, ill-mannered, or insecure, none of which are desirable.

DANCING WITH THE TRANSFORMERS

Any guy who's serious about meeting and dating Transformers should learn to salsa. It ain't easy because Latin guys have been doing it since they were kids and show-off on the dance floor. But non-Latin men score big points by taking some lessons, getting out there, stepping on a few toes, and having fun. Perfection isn't necessary.

HABITAT: (Salsa) dance club or lesson; (private) party; Cuban café, cigar room, or restaurant; office building; college campus; political event; Catholic Church; beach.

LOCATION: Abundant in south FL, especially Westchester, Hialeah, Coral Terrace, West Miami, University Park, Olympia Heights, Tamiami, Hialeah Gardens, Medley, Sweetwater, Palm Springs North, Miami Lakes, Kendall Lakes, Fontainebleau, Miami, Coral Gables, Kendall, and Miami Beach. Common in West New York. Somewhat common in northern NJ.

MIGRATION: Somewhat migratory.

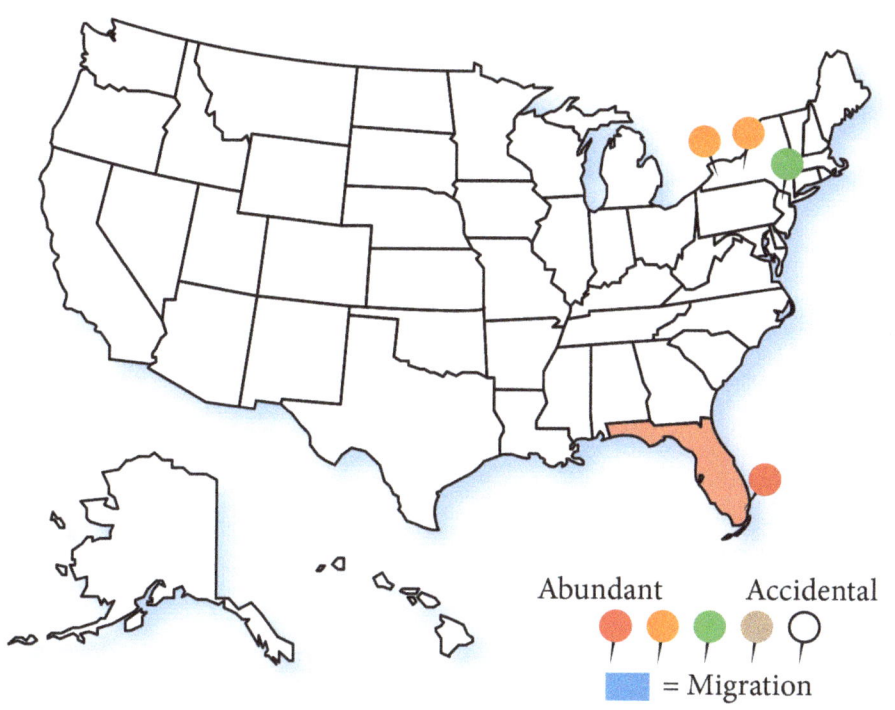

Abundant   Accidental

■ = Migration

PERUSIAN™
(Peruvian American)

APPEARANCE: Ethnically ambiguous fusion of Mestizo, Amerindian, and Spanish descent, but occasionally pure or mixed Chinese or Japanese, part Afro-Peruvian, or even Arab. Normally has more of a cylindrical than hourglass shape, with a relatively wide waist, a long butt, short legs, and naturally small to medium-sized breasts. Usually rather slender or average-sized but the cylinder gets considerably wider at times. Often appears top-heavy after a boob job because her booty isn't plump enough to balance things out. Other field marks include a relatively big head, roundish face, high cheekbones, slightly slanted eyes, large mouth, slightly "tosco" (rough) nose and lips, and light brown, bronzed, or olive-tinged skin.

1/3 ASS

If you see a woman who's practically 1/3 ass (vertically speaking) with a distinctively cylindrical shape, big head, short legs, (light) brown skin similar to other Latinas, and *slightly slanted eyes*, chances are she's a Perusian.

NOTABLES

Daniella Alonso (1/2 *Nuyorican*), Silvana Arias, Juana Burga Cervera, Alexis Amore, Isis Taylor, and Natalie Vertiz.

BEHAVIOR: Cheerful and easy-going most of the time but hot-tempered (if her man checks out another woman) and prone to mood swings. Humble, traditional, and conservative in many ways. Often straightforward and religious (predominantly Catholic). Loves to eat great food (including ceviche), drink pisco, listen to huayño, and in some cases, surf. Generally well-educated, and hardworking (if necessary) but nevertheless prefers to marry a financially stable guy and stay at home with the kids.

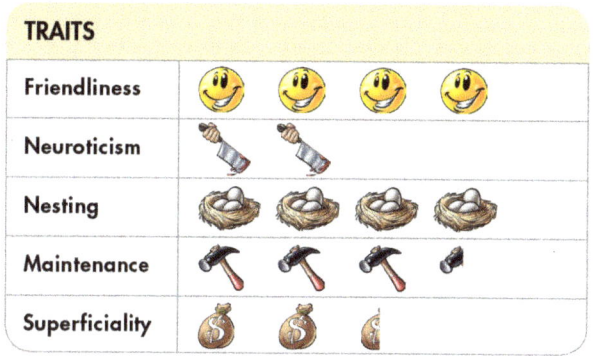
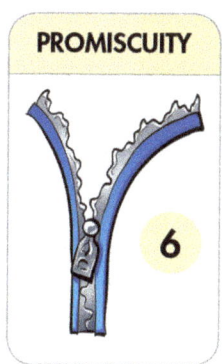

SONG: Loves to sing (the same old Latino summer hits) even if her voice sucks. Laughs frequently.

THE HUMAN LIE DETECTOR

The Perusian places a high value on sincerity and observes men closely to see if they measure up. She may also (secretly) monitor a guy's text messages, emails, voicemails, and/or social media profiles for evidence of dishonesty. If she catches him in a lie, he's toast.

MATING: Romantic, sensual, and aggressive in pursuit of eligible bachelors but possessive, jealous (at times), and cautious about pre-marital sex until she trusts a guy in a committed relationship. Wild and up for anything in the sack once she does. Known to wait three to six weeks before closing the deal.

MAGNETS: Attracted mainly to white, Latin, and Middle-Eastern gentlemen who treat her like a princess and make her feel like one, especially if they're well-educated and financially stable. Strongly prefers (ostensibly) sincere men of high moral character. Rarely resorts to blatant gold digging but occasionally tries to outsmart the system in search of a visa.

HABITAT: Beach; restaurant; hotel; (dance) club or lounge; beauty salon; office building; pool; (private) party.

LOCATION: Common to somewhat common in New Jersey, especially East Newark (borough), Harrison, Paterson, Kearny, and Prospect Park. Somewhat common to casual in Florida, especially Hammocks, Virginia Gardens, Bay Harbor Islands, Doral, Key Biscayne, North Bay Village, Ojus, Kendal, and Kendal Lakes; and New York, especially Port Chester, Glen Cove, Rye, Elmsford, and White Plains.

MIGRATION: Migratory.

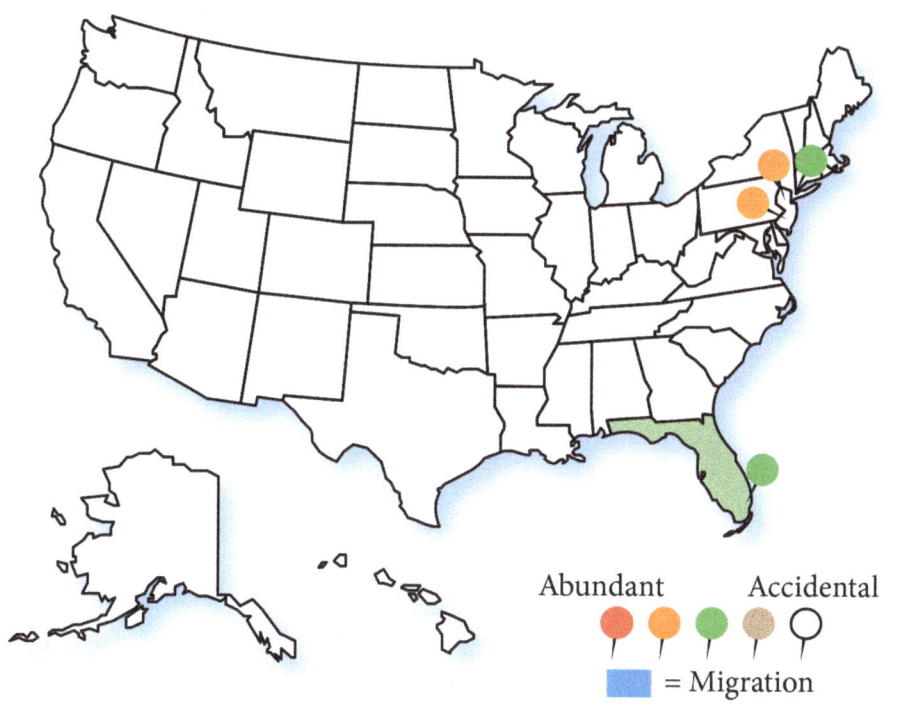

CINNAMON SWIRL™
(Dominican American – Florida)

76 • WHY LATINAS GET THE GUY

APPEARANCE: Café latte or café mocha skin tone because approximately 73% of the Dominican population is mixed-race (black and something else), another 11% or so is black only, and many are tri-racial (with Taíno or Native American ancestry). Other field marks include: A small waist followed by a round booty on a short to medium-sized frame; an oval-shaped head (with puffy cheeks); long, naturally coarse black hair; full lips; big eyes; and a (slightly) wide or large nose. Breast size varies but implants are common. Nose jobs too. Usually well-groomed and fashionable. Carefully checks her outfit and accessories to ensure that everything matches before she leaves the house. Likes makeup, even if it's not necessary, and tight, sexy clothing to show off her body, even if she's fat.

NOTABLES

Evelyn Jimenez, Aimee Carrero, Mirtha Michelle, Dania Ramirez, Iliana Ramirez, and Amelia Vega.

SHE'S DOMINICAN, NOT BLACK

The Cinnamon Swirl often defines race by skin tone, including rubia (even if she's not blond), india, morena, and various in-between tones, but rarely refers to herself as black. If she doesn't do it, neither should you.

BEHAVIOR: Highly charismatic and gregarious, but stubborn and close-minded now and then. Drives as if traffic laws are optional and honks way too much at intersections. Often religious (Roman Catholic), moralistic, and superstitious but seldom boring. Usually from a large, close-knit, middle-class family that immigrated to Florida for greater freedom and economic opportunity. Tends to be reasonably well-educated, skilled, and entrepreneurial. Loves to sing (even on public transportation), dance, party, and watch baseball.

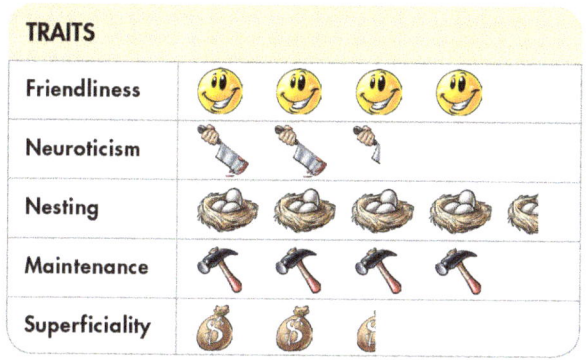

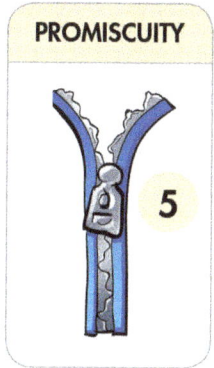

CHARISMA ENOUGH FOR TWO

Good luck finding a woman in the American field with more natural charisma than the Cinnamon Swirl. She knows how to have fun under almost any circumstances.

SONG: Chatty, gossipy, and highly expressive, especially among friends, but noisy and whiny at times. Giggles, smiles, and jokes around frequently. Peppers her Spanish with plenty of slang and abbreviations.

MATING: Ostensibly sweet, innocent, and loving but often secretly somewhat calculating, manipulative, and high-maintenance. Tends to be loving, loyal, and nurturing but equally demanding and dependent, especially after marriage. Sensual but rarely promiscuous because she prefers a serious relationship to casual sex. Wild in bed once there's a commitment but somewhat inhibited otherwise. Known to wait three dates to two months before closing the deal.

MAGNETS: Attracted mainly to tall, family-oriented white guys (with blue eyes), especially if they're romantic, respectful, and successful. Occasionally dates other types — especially non-Dominican Latinos — but seldom drawn to black men or others with darker skin tones. Often turned off by jealous or possessive behavior.

WITH COMPLIMENTS

The Cinnamon Swirl is used to hearing piropos (compliments) from Dominican men and expects the same from other guys, who shouldn't hold back. She loves the validation and wants to feel appreciated by the opposite sex.

HABITAT: Dance club; party; (Dominican) beauty salon; Catholic Church; networking event; bar; restaurant.

LOCATION: Common to somewhat common in FL, especially Miami Gardens, Country Club, Carol City, Fontainebleau, Hialeah Gardens, Yeehaw Junction, Opa-Locka, South Miami Heights, Richmond West, West Little River, Virginia Gardens, El Portal, Miramar, North Bay Village, North Miami Beach, and Miami. Casual in NJ, NY, MA, and RI.

MIGRATION: Migratory.

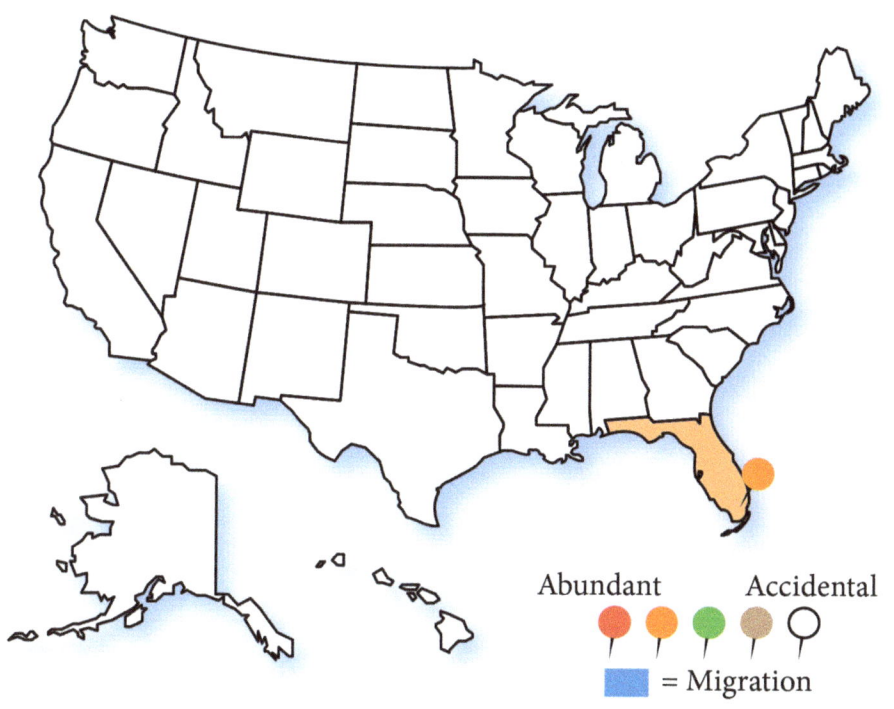

Abundant Accidental

= Migration

WHY LATINAS GET THE GUY • 79

BEAUTY CALL™
(Dominican American – Northeast)

APPEARANCE: Look for casual (but sexy) clothing, natural breasts (most of the time), good grooming, and other field marks similar to the *Cinnamon Swirl* in Florida, including a café mocha or café latte complexion, naturally coarse black hair, small waist, round booty, petite to medium-sized frame, a (slightly) big or wide nose, and full lips. Also tends to have an oval-shaped head and big, expressive eyes.

NOTABLES

Adriana Diaz, Claudette Lali, Christina Mendez, Zoe Saldana (1/2 *Nuyorican*), Rosanna Tavarez, Omahyra Mota, Julissa Bermudez, and Miracles Espinal.

BEHAVIOR: Frequently visits or owns a Dominican beauty salon that caters primarily to Dominicans and other Latin American chicks. Tends to be energetic, spunky, and cheerful but lives, works, and socializes mainly with other Latinos, especially Dominicans. Normally comes from a family that resided in a poor rural town or urban ghetto in the Dominican Republic before immigrating to the United States. Typically hardworking, proud, family-oriented, and (somewhat) socially conservative. Often urban and inadequately educated, but there are an increasing number of exceptions. Loves to dance, party, and play.

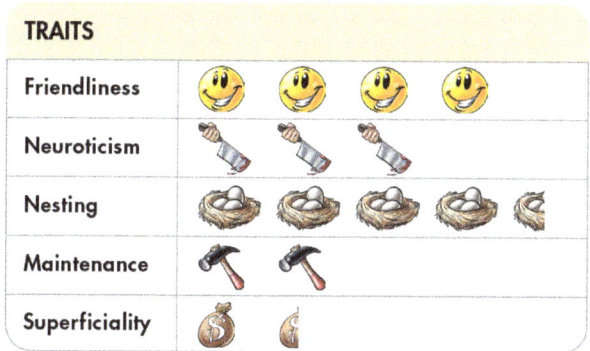
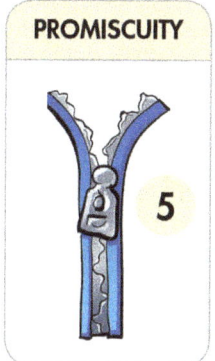

SONG: Verbose and opinionated but often somewhat inarticulate. Frequently curses and resorts to street slang. Gossipy, loud, and whiny at times.

WHAT THE F*CK?

Zoe Saldana, the pretty *Beauty Call/Nuyorican* actress who starred in the movie "Avatar" as a half-naked blue girl, "says 'fuck' slightly less often than Caroline Kennedy says 'you know'," according to *Esquire* magazine. When asked about her ethnic Dominican background, she replied: "I hate that fucking question." She also noted: "That's why I try not to drink caffeine — it really fucks me up." Think twice before bringing this one home to meet your mother without a dress rehearsal.

MATING: Inclined to marry young and have kids right away because family matters most. Relatively low-maintenance for a lively, hot-blooded Latina who works hard and copes with plenty of stress on a daily basis. Known to wait three weeks to two months before closing the deal.

MAGNETS: Attracted predominantly to Dominican/Latin, black, and swarthy Southern European men but open to dating other types too, especially if they're cool, confident, or charismatic in some way. Far more interested in love, family, and (financial) security than luxury.

HABITAT: Dominican beauty salon; bodega; grocery store; garment shop; city restaurant or club; private party or any other gathering of friends and family.

LOCATION: Common to somewhat common in New York, especially Haverstraw, Sleepy Hollow, the Bronx, Manhattan, Washington Heights, Freeport (village), Copiague, Brentwood, and New York City; New Jersey, especially Perth Amboy, Passaic, Union City, Paterson, West New York, New Brunswick, Weehawken, North Bergen, Prospect Park, Guttenburg, Jersey City, and Hackensack; Massachusetts, especially Lawrence, Lynn, and Salem; and Providence, Rhode Island.

MIGRATION: Somewhat nonmigratory (except for trips to the Dominican Republic).

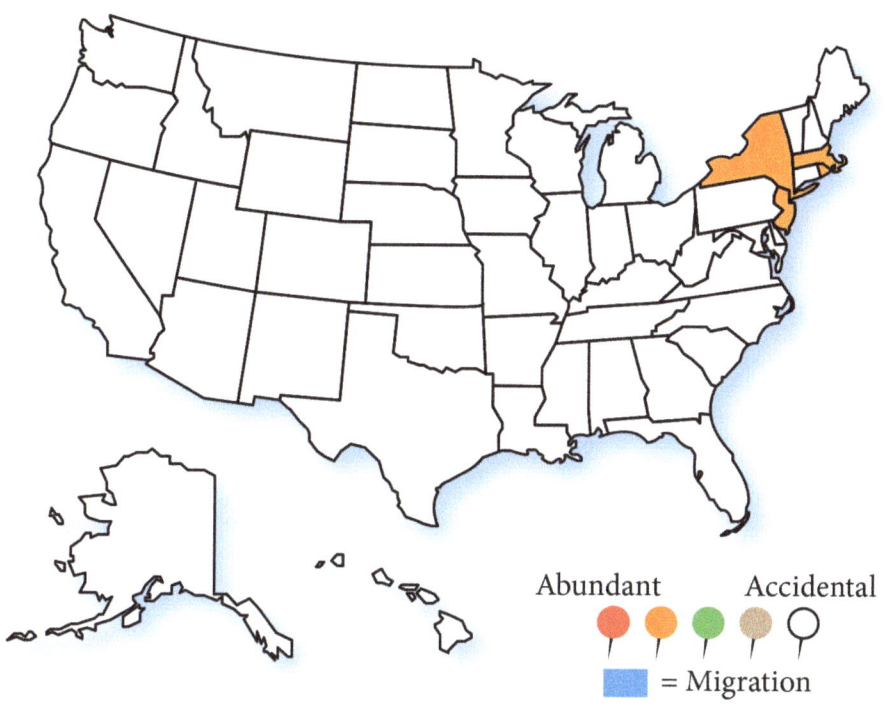

Abundant   Accidental

= Migration

WHY LATINAS GET THE GUY • 83

PUPUSA™
(Salvadoran American)

APPEARANCE: The Pupusa [poo-poo-suh] is recognizable by her (somewhat) auburn-colored skin, big eyelashes, full lips, slightly wide or big nose on a round or oval-shaped face, brown hair, brown eyes, high cheekbones, and other features revealing some native Indian ancestry. Tends to be petite, average-sized or (slightly) overweight, with naturally medium-sized to large breasts. Normally takes it easy on the makeup — except for the eyes — and jewelry. Inclined to prefer simple, casual clothing over fancy or flashy attire.

LESS IS MORE

The Pupusa tends to wear less ostentatious clothing and accessories than the Mexican American *Taco Belle*, if you're having trouble telling the difference.

BEHAVIOR: Hardworking — Salvadorans are often called "the Germans of Central America" — tough as nails, and religious (mainly Roman Catholic). Bright and optimistic but tends to sacrifice education and career to start a family at the earliest opportunity. More or less friendly but temperamental, cliquish, and bitchy at times. Loves to party and enjoy life but occasionally associates with Salvadoran thugs or gang members.

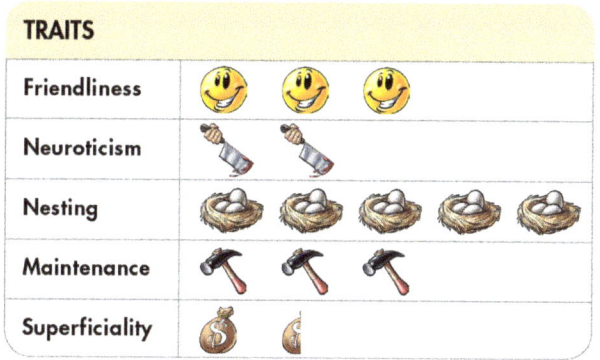
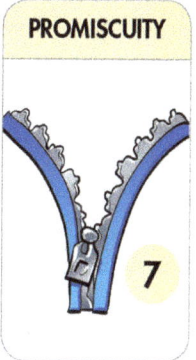

THINK TWICE

Mess with the Pupusa and she'll see to it that you never make that mistake again.

SONG: Speaks with a sultry slur. Frequently uses profanity, especially when angry or agitated, and likes to say "Bos!" (Hey you!). Often animated and loud.

MATING: Known for being a great lover who gets a man in over his head before he knows what hit him. Tends to marry young, have a few kids, and get fat. Typically sends quite a bit of (his) money back to family in El Salvador. Known to wait one date to one month before closing the deal.

PUPUSA ADDICTION

Countless guys develop an addiction to Pupusa every year and end up hooked for life. Sleep with her in moderation or start saving for your kids' education right now.

MAGNETS: Attracted mainly to honest, hardworking men who know how to have fun. Open to dating outside her close-knit ethnic community but usually ends up marrying a Salvadoran or Mexican guy anyway. (Note: The Pupusa and *Taco Belle* often compete for eligible bachelors and like to claim that their men don't cross over, but it happens all the time and results in a lot of Salvadoran-Mexican marriages.)

HABITAT: Any Salvadoran event or party; nightclub; dance club; university; service industry job.

LOCATION: Common in the Washington metropolitan area of Washington D.C., Maryland, and Northern Virginia, especially Langley Park, Adelphi, Chillum, Brentwood, and Silver Spring, MD; Seven Corners, Bailey's Crossroads, and Herndon, VA; New York, especially New Cassel, Brentwood, North Bay Shore Hempstead, Huntington Station, Inwood, Uniondale, Freeport, and Roosevelt; and California, especially Mendota, Colma, the greater Los Angeles area, and the San Francisco Bay area. Somewhat common in northern New Jersey, Houston, Austin, Dallas, Chicago, and Chelsea, Massachusetts.

MIGRATION: Migratory.

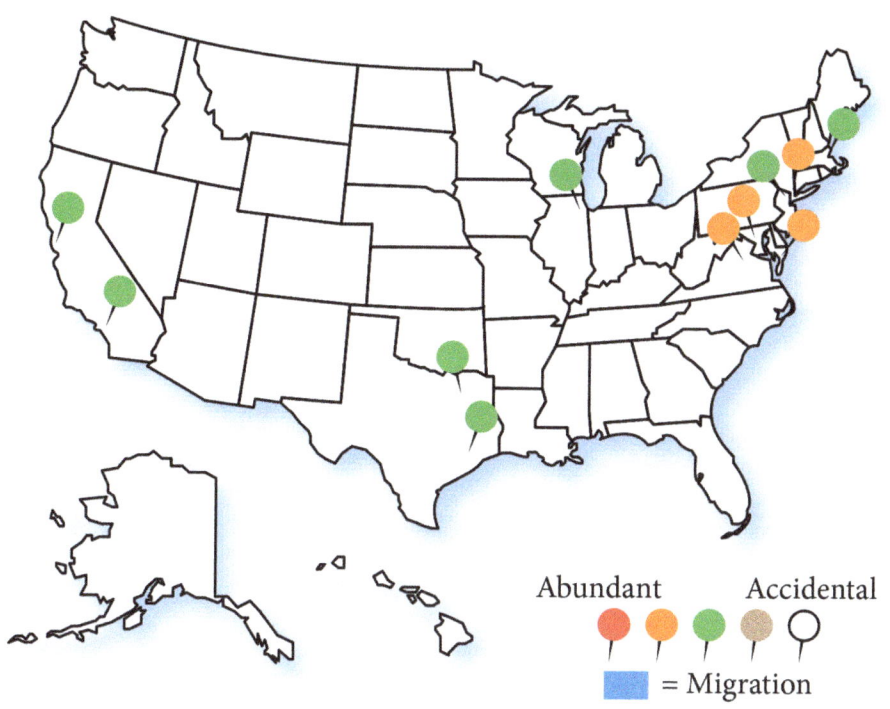

Abundant   Accidental

= Migration

HOTEMALAN™
(Guatemalan American)

APPEARANCE: Look for a compact, pint-sized body made to dance all night long, with small, perky breasts and a tight (at least slightly curvy) little butt. Typically balloons to average or plus-sized as soon as she has a child. Other field marks include distinctively Mayan facial features, such as high, wide cheekbones; big, slightly slanted, dark brown eyes; a flat, long, hawkish nose with a high, flat bridge; cocoa-colored skin tone; and straight black hair. Tends to dress sexy but conservatively and not wear a lot of makeup.

NOTABLES

Pam Rodriguez (1/2 *La Guitarra*), Martita Albarracin, Kalucha Chacon, Gabriela Salvado, Carmen Ramos, Denise Galindo (1/2 *Taco Belle*), and Claudia Rocio.

BEHAVIOR: Pleasant, serene, family-oriented, and traditional in many ways. Tends to be (reasonably) intelligent and understand the importance of a solid education. Often hardworking and somewhat religious (mainly Catholic).

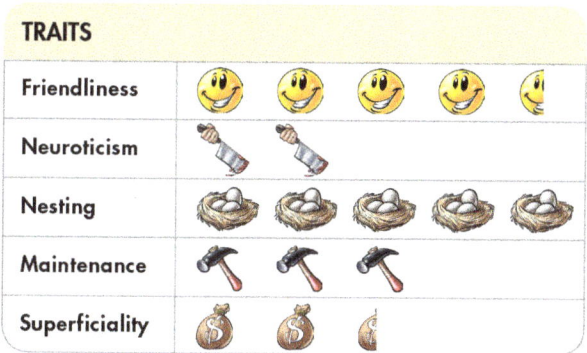

SONG: Relatively quiet and subdued around strangers but expressive and animated with close friends and family. Gabby and opinionated but rarely loud or pushy.

MATING: Mildly conservative but sensual, amorous, and red-hot behind closed doors. Normally doesn't sleep around, but not holding out for marriage either and will go for it occasionally if the chemistry is right. Womanly but really feisty, tough, and highly demanding at times. Known to wait one night to one month before closing the deal.

ONLY YOU

The Hotemalan doesn't jump into bed with every guy she dates, but she may move things along pretty quickly for a good man who shows sincere interest in whatever she cares about and makes her feel like the most important person in his world for a while.

MAGNETS: Drawn mainly to Latin or white guys who are financially stable, family-oriented, ostensibly honest, and relatively handsome (with a nice smile and beautiful eyes). Seldom dates Asian or black men.

HABITAT: (Latin) dance club and/or bar; soccer game; college or university; poolside; beach; church.

LOCATION: Abundant to common in Georgetown, DE; Ellijay, GA; Brewster, NY; and Langley Park, MD. Common to casual in many other places across the country, including but not limited to: Green Forest, AR; Chamblee, Buena Vista, Trion, Cedartown, and Canton, GA; Collinsville, AL; Indiantown, Lake Worth, Immokalee, Tice, Mangonia Park, and Homestead, FL; Mount Kisco, Jamesport, Spring Valley, and Port Chester, NY; Central Falls, RI; Schuyler and Lexington, NE; Morganton, NC; Fairview, NJ; Monterey, TN; and Los Angeles, CA. Rare in the Great Plains states and large sections of the Western United States.

MIGRATION: Somewhat migratory (if single); homebody (after marriage).

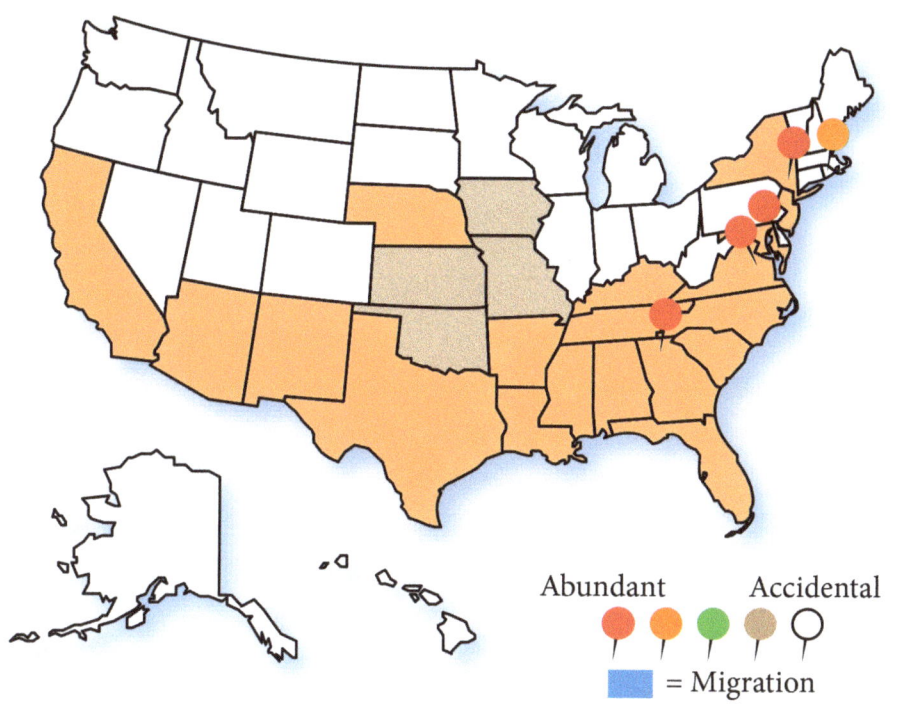

OH YEAH, THERE'S MORE.

For free no-BS dating and relationship advice,
visit **JoeBovino.com**.

CHAPTER FOUR

AMERICAN WOMEN:
If She Looks Like a Man, Talks Like a Man, and Sleeps Around Like a Man, She's Probably an American Woman

"Marriage is like a tense, unfunny version of Everybody Loves Raymond, only it doesn't last 22 minutes. It lasts forever."

— Pete (Character), Knocked Up (2007)

American Chickspotting: What You See Is What You Get

If you studied the profiles on America's Latinas in Chapter Three, you should notice an immediate improvement in your chicaspotting skills. (You're welcome.) But you can't fully understand the allure of Latin-American women until you check out the competition. So, in this chapter, we'll compare and contrast profiles on 14 (mostly regional) subcultures of fully assimilated American women. (For more comprehensive coverage, consult my award-winning *Field Guide to Chicks of the United States*.)

Does the contrast shed some light on why Latinas get the guy?

I say, on balance, it does. But you be the judge.

The American chick species profiled below are as follows:

1) 49er (San Francisco, CA)
2) Sili-Clone (Orange County, CA)
3) Star Burst (California)
4) Perfect 6 (Seattle, WA)
5) Bigger Better Deal (Aspen, CO)
6) Hole in One (Las Vegas, NV)
7) South Beeotch (Miami Beach, FL)
8) Boca Bitch (Boca Raton, FL)
9) So Ho' (New York, NY)
10) Bronx Tail (Northeast)
11) Hurt Rocker (Emo)
12) Brooding Barfly (Hipster)
13) Big Bang (Rubenesque)
14) Cougar (Sexual Predator)

As in Chapter Three, each species profile includes a behavioral trait chart and promiscuity zipper.

Here's how they work:

- **Friendliness** (with one smiley face as least friendly and five as most): Friendliness refers to how approachable and gregarious she is, how much she laughs and smiles, and how quickly she warms to strangers.

- **Neuroticism** (with one bloody cleaver as least neurotic and five as most): Neuroticism refers to how stressed out, anxious, or potentially psychotic she is or appears to be.

- **Nesting** (with one bird's nest as least interested in marriage and kids, and five as most): Nesting refers to how determined and likely she is to get married young, have kids, and settle down—but also reflects the priority that she tends to place on family, and how often she sacrifices career to be a homemaker or stay-at-home mom.

- **Maintenance** (with one hammer as lowest maintenance and five as highest): Maintenance refers to how much love, attention, or support she needs to feel satisfied in a relationship.

- **Superficiality** (with one bag of money as least superficial and five as most): Superficiality refers to how many purely superficial considerations (e.g., money, looks, or ethnicity) play into mate selection and serve as powerful chick magnets.

- **Promiscuity** (with one, zipped up, as least promiscuous and ten, unzipped, as most): Promiscuity refers to how likely she is to sleep around and have casual sex while single.

Now let's go American chickspotting.

Brace yourself …

49ER™
(San Francisco, CA)

96 • WHY LATINAS GET THE GUY

APPEARANCE: The San Francisco 49er (a "4" who thinks she's a "9"), also known as the Mission Hipster, combines styles in search of a uniquely hip, bohemian or artsy look. Funky (sun) glasses and hat, tattoos, piercings, ripped (skinny) jeans, t-shirts (with slogans), long skirts and blouses, (Birkenstock) sandals, and homemade jewelry and accessories are popular. Seldom wears fur or leather. Shaving — anywhere — is optional, as is underwear. Freeboobing is common. Normally pale, with little or no makeup or attention to her hair. Occasionally gets a short bowl cut or dreadlocks. Decent figure, but a little flabby here and there.

BEHAVIOR: Cozies up to hipsters, bohemians, and other like-minded individuals but relatively cold and unwelcoming to others, especially yuppies and prepsters. "Artistic" (broadly defined), bookish, and well-traveled. Rebellious, angst-ridden, and politically liberal but often apathetic, ideologically rigid, or nerdy. Enjoys riding her (track) bike everywhere. Likely smokes weed or uses other drugs but stays healthy with organic foods, vegetarianism, and non-traditional athletic activities.

TRAITS			
Friendliness	😃	😃	
Neuroticism	🧂	🧂	🧂
Nesting	🪺		
Maintenance	🔨	🔨	🔨
Superficiality	💰	💰	💰

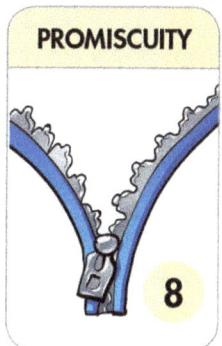

PROMISCUITY 8

THE LITMUS TEST

Active membership in the Democratic Party and associated interest groups is a trusty chick magnet in San Francisco, America's most liberal city. Any guy who's socially conservative or even moderately Republican should expect to fail the 49er's political litmus test on a regular basis.

SONG: Highly opinionated and sarcastic but cynical, combative, and seemingly bipolar at times.

MATING: Open to casual sex with a suitable partner. Often lesbian, bisexual or bi-curious, and convinced that she's hotter than she really is. Religiosity is usually a turn-off but spirituality can be an asset. Anything goes in bed because she rarely has hang-ups about sex or her body, even if she's unattractive. Known to wait for up to three dates before closing the deal.

LOWER STANDARDS AND PRACTICES

The 49er isn't prudish, but a guy should be prepared to lower his standards and take what he can get. On the bright side, he's more likely to end up in a threesome in San Francisco than most other American cities.

MAGNETS: Normally attracted to smug hipster guys with an artsy passion project, hobby, or (if necessary) "job;" solid liberal arts education; environmental consciousness; and lots of free time to hang out. Other politically correct men who really "get" her and fit in with her friends also have a considerable edge. The rest can forget it.

HABITAT: Dolores Park; dive bar; bike path; thrift store; yoga, belly dancing, hula-hooping, or meditation class; medical marijuana store; artsy café; lesbian or bisexual event; festivals (e.g., Burning Man); leftist political rally or protest; Trader Joe's; independent movie theater; thrift store; bookstore.

LOCATION: Abundant in the Mission, Noe Valley, Potrero Hill, and SoMa (south of Market) sections of San Francisco, CA, with its unfavorable single girl-to-guy ratio. Somewhat common to casual in other parts of the city, neighboring cities (e.g., Santa Cruz, Marin), and Seattle, WA.

MIGRATION: Migratory.

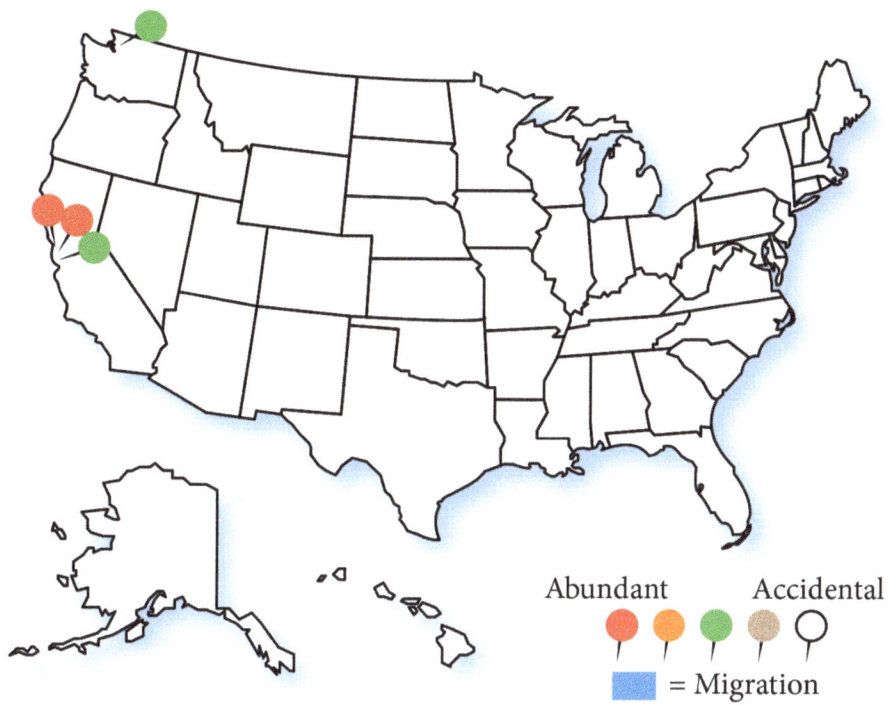

Abundant   Accidental

◯ = Migration

WHY LATINAS GET THE GUY • 99

SILI-CLONE™
(Orange County, CA)

APPEARANCE: Cross between Malibu Barbie and Jenna Jameson. Tends to have straight, fried (platinum) blond hair; an orangey tan; huge, rock-hard fake boobs; and a shapely, tight butt. Often size 2 or less and relatively fit. Other field marks include fake nails; swollen lips; lots of makeup; a big wedding ring on the wrong finger; a flashy, studded-out designer outfit — pink is a popular color — or revealing top and jeans; expensive shoes; and the trendiest brand-name accessories.

BEHAVIOR: Saccharine sweet and sociable but conniving, pretentious, and pampered. Nonchalant and convivial but insecure, unstable, and needy at times. Normally somewhat socially conservative and ostensibly religious. Often supports her carefree lifestyle with cash from rich parents, a sugar daddy, or large alimony and child support payments. Loves to sunbathe, go boating, socialize, and shop.

TRAITS					
Friendliness	😃	😃	😃		
Neuroticism	💊	💊	💊	💊	
Nesting	🪺	🪺	🪺		
Maintenance	🔨	🔨	🔨	🔨	🔨
Superficiality	💰	💰	💰	💰	💰

PROMISCUITY: 7

SONG: Laughs too hard at corny jokes by wealthy guys, especially if she's young. Highly catty and gossipy. Common expressions include: "She's so 909." (Translation: That skank lives in a less affluent county covered by the 909 area code, such as far eastern LA County, southeastern San Bernardino County, or portions of Riverside County).

MATING: High-maintenance gold digger (in her sexual prime) who competes fiercely against other Sili-Clones. Too conservative and image conscious to be overtly promiscuous or slutty — before a few lavish dates anyway — but horny and not above using sex to reel-in a good catch. Craves attention, photo ops, and social networking "friends." Often resorts to desperate measures or doubles as a *Cougar* by her mid-30s. Known to wait for up to three dates before closing the deal.

BATTLE OF THE CLONES

Young Sili-Clones in their 20s and early 30s shamelessly hang out with wealthy lizards in their 50s and 60s, especially if the economy is bad. Older Sili-Clones are seriously interested in these ballers too and hot enough to compete for them after a little nip/tuck.

MAGNETS: Strongly attracted to ostensibly rich white guys in their 30s to 60s, even if they're otherwise unattractive or sleazy. Occasionally dates non-white men if they're equally loaded and generous. Hooks up casually with other types every now and then because she can only go so long without sex. Ridiculously starstruck when celebrities venture behind the Orange Curtain (i.e., the border of Orange County, CA).

HABITAT: Shiny mall; luxury specialty retail department store; country club; yacht or other boat; beauty or tanning salon; upscale bar (for happy hour); ritzy nightclub; five-star restaurant or hotel (poolside); pristine beach; outdoor café; art walk or gallery; charity event; ultimate fighting function. Occasionally found in (Christian) church.

LOCATION: Abundant in Newport Beach, CA (where they glam it up Hollywood style), Laguna Beach, CA, and other affluent parts of the "OC" (Orange County, CA). Somewhat common in nearby Huntington Beach, CA (where they glam it down), Costa Mesa, and Seal Beach. Casual in other parts of the OC. Migrates periodically to Aspen and Vail, CO; Las Vegas; New York City; Los Angeles; and other baller hotspots.

MIGRATION: Frequent flyer.

WHY LATINAS GET THE GUY

STAR BURST™
(African American – California)

APPEARANCE: Curvaceous but lean, athletic and toned, with a super-thin waistline, track-star booty, muscular legs, relatively thick hips, and medium-sized breasts (which would be larger if she weren't so fit or got a boob job). Normally has treated black or dark brown hair with long extensions. Facial features tend to include a relatively wide nose, naturally full lips, and prominent cheekbones. Outfit generally consists of hyper-trendy or sporty-casual clothing with lots of accessories. Frequently sighted wearing a skin-tight "tube" dress, skinny jeans that hug the curves, and heels. Occasionally rocks a fedora, plaid shirt, or something more urban. Skin tone varies from dark to light brown.

BEHAVIOR: Highly independent networking diva (with at least two club promoters on speed dial). Relatively friendly, laid-back and approachable but picky and suspicious because she has to cut through so much BS from black men. Often manages considerable stress and drama on a daily basis but conceals it well. Free-spirited but often religious (mainly Christian), judgmental, and somewhat socially conservative, especially if she's older.

TRAITS						PROMISCUITY
Friendliness	😀	😀	😀	😀		8.5
Neuroticism	🔨	🔨	🔨			
Nesting	🪺	🪺	🪺			
Maintenance	🔨	🔨	🔨	🔨	🔨	
Superficiality	💰	💰	💰	💰		

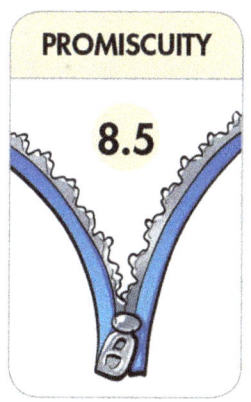

SONG: Adapts her song to suit the environment (e.g., the "hood" versus the office). Expressive, with a big, easy laugh. Opinionated but backs it up and rarely becomes antagonistic. (This is California, after all.) Bilingual at times. Enjoys intellectually stimulating conversation because she needs to know what's up.

MATING: Serial dater. Time is valuable and dating is a professional sport (or business), but sex is often just another day at the gym. Horny and selectively promiscuous but ready to be swept off her feet. Always wondering what you can do for her. Tends to live beyond her means to impress guys who can help her achieve the (financial) stability she can't attain on her own. Loves to be seen with a man who complements her style and supports her socially. Known to wait for three dates (more or less) before closing the deal.

MAGNETS: A guy overall health and appearance are just as important as the kind of car he drives. Normally drawn to black men but open to dating any alpha male who approaches confidently, pays the bills (his and hers), dresses in style, and maintains a social network of attractive, well-connected friends. Well-rounded, multi-dimensional guys (who know more than the "thug" life, for example) also have an edge.

FRONT MAN

Faking and fronting still work on the Star Burst, but guys shouldn't try too hard to make an impression because she's a fast-moving target. Just enjoy her company while it lasts and watch her go without freaking out.

HABITAT: Restaurant that doesn't rip you off (e.g., Cheesecake Factory, TGI Friday's, El Torito); nightclub or bar (that's popular with Star Bursts and eligible bachelors); private party; mall; concert; sporting event; church; (black) networking function; theater (playing a film starring black actors).

LOCATION: Approximately 9% of African Americans live in the West, but the Star Burst is abundant in California (the nation's most populous state), with the fifth largest African-American population in the country. Oakland and Los Angeles (with the epicenter at Hollywood and Highland) are real hotspots.

MIGRATION: Migratory.

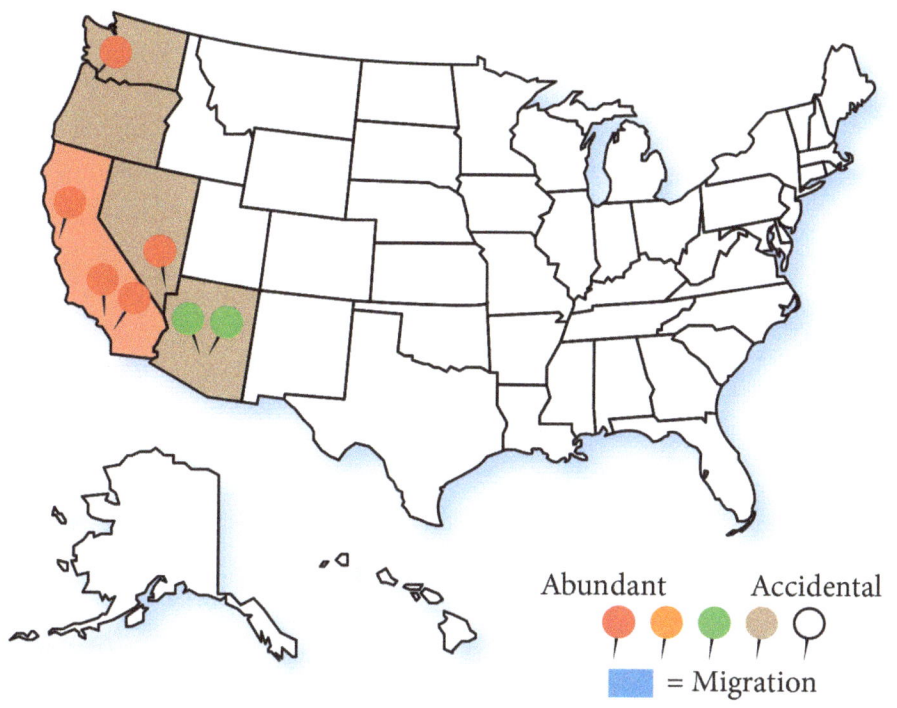

Abundant　Accidental

= Migration

PERFECT 6™
(Seattle, WA)

108 • WHY LATINAS GET THE GUY

APPEARANCE: This earthy chick is rarely hotter than a 6 but harder to pick up than a 10 in many other American cities. Usually has an average body with smooth, pale skin (from all the rain) but pays less attention to hair, makeup, and personal grooming than most American women, resulting in noticeably hairy body parts on the proud "granola" or hippie version. Inclined to wear fleece sweaters, T-shirts, jeans, Birkenstocks (with socks), a Gore-Tex storm jacket, and other stuff from North Face, Lands' End, REI, or Eddie Bauer. The end result tends to be bland, nondescript, or unkempt.

CHICK OR DUDE?

The Perfect 6 looks eerily similar to the male equivalent, making it difficult to distinguish between them at times. This is especially true if she doubles as a *Hurt Rocker* from the thriving "emo" (emotional) and indie music scene in Seattle.

BEHAVIOR: Introverted, socially awkward, and relatively unwelcoming. Normally well-read, highly educated, and progressive but coolly aloof, cliquish, and class-conscious. Also tends to be noticeably edgy, whiny, or melancholy because of all the gloomy weather. Enjoys neighborhood cafes and outdoor activities (e.g., camping, kayaking), weather-permitting. Often politically liberal and non-religious.

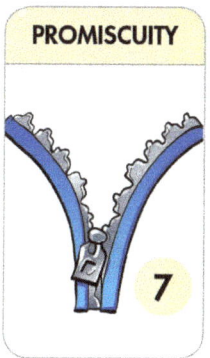

THE SEATTLE FREEZE

Guys who aren't from the Northwest tend to get a frosty reception — known as the "Seattle freeze" — because the Perfect 6 is even colder when it comes to outsiders.

SONG: Chatty online. Offline ... not so much. Sticks to the keyboard because Seattle has a high percentage of online daters. That's where the action is — in cyberspace.

MATING: All those cute coffee shops don't translate into much sexual energy because the Perfect 6 is rarely flirtatious, relatively serious, and extremely picky. The degree of difficulty increases even further if she's bi-curious, lesbian, or angry at men in general for some reason. Known to wait for three dates before closing the deal.

MAGNETS: Attracted to wealthy local (tech) guys who know how to chill out and spend money on average-looking American women. Also drawn to "real" men, rugged outdoorsmen, and successful artists who have something interesting to say and aren't holding out for Jessica Simpson. Unlikely to judge or hassle guys who smoke, drink beer, or do drugs because she probably does (or has) too.

HABITAT: Local coffee shop or casual restaurant/bar; dive bar; hotel bar; bookstore; University Village; Bellevue Square; lake; park; music venue.

LOCATION: Abundant in Seattle, WA. Common in Tacoma, WA. Migrates occasionally to ritzy Bellevue, WA but gets pulled over for driving an old, ugly car. May migrate to Alaska in search of a high-paying temp job.

THE PERFECT SAUSAGE

The unfavorable single chick-to-guy ratio in the Seattle area presents another obstacle for men in search of a Perfect 6. Even accounting for all the gays on "Capitol Hill" and elsewhere, it's still a sausage fest.

MIGRATION: Somewhat nonmigratory.

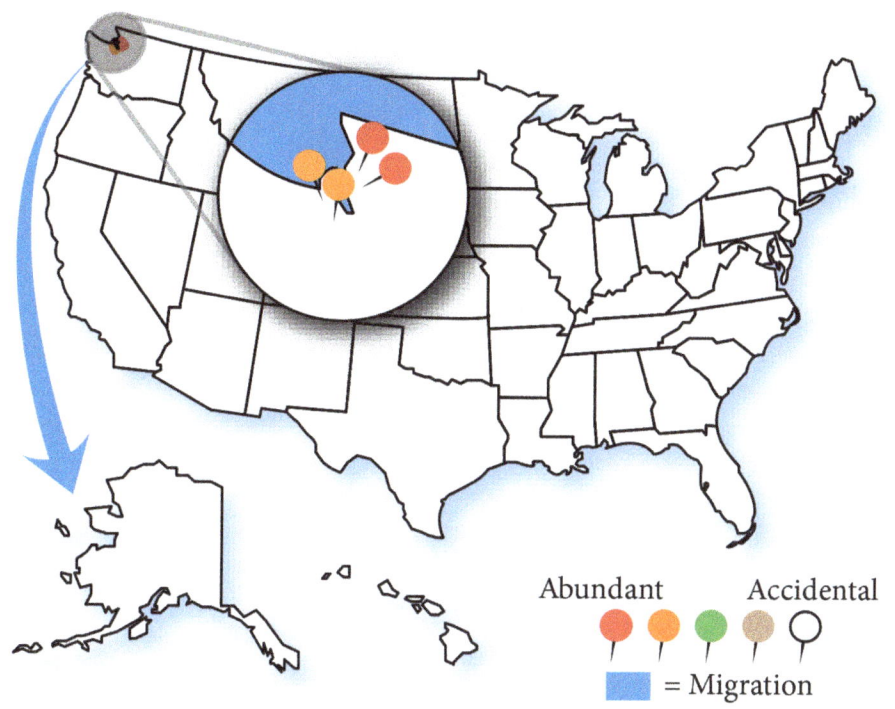

Abundant Accidental

= Migration

BIGGER BETTER DEAL™
(Aspen, CO)

APPEARANCE: The Bigger Better Deal (or "BBD") always puts her best face forward, even if it's barely recognizable after all the cosmetic surgery. She tends to have a large (fake) rack on a relatively slender frame, noticeably strong legs (from ski season prep exercises), optional Donald Duck lips (from collagen), and taut skin (from Botox and fillers). Wears brand-name clothing and accessories and plenty of fur.

BEHAVIOR: Spends lots of money on fancy ski clothes. Works the après-ski circuit early and often. Well-traveled, cultured, and shrewd. Friendly and welcoming because the Aspen crowd is close-knit and exclusive but (somewhat) snobbish, pretentious, elitist, and/or spoiled. Often prefers skiing to snowboarding if she's over 30, which is usually the case.

TRAITS					
Friendliness	😊	😊	😊	😊	
Neuroticism	💊	💊	💊	💊	
Nesting	🪺	🪺	🪺		
Maintenance	🔨	🔨	🔨	🔨	
Superficiality	💰	💰	💰	💰	💰

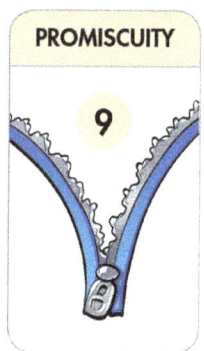

PROMISCUITY
9

SONG: Garrulous and opinionated, especially about shopping, vacationing, money, and the best places to see and be seen. Consummate networker and name-dropper. Always sexting because phone service is so poor. Common probing questions to sniff out the green include: "Who do you know in Aspen?" "Where do you summer?" and "How did you get here?" (Jet-fishing)

MATING: Promiscuous, materialistic, and high maintenance. Keen on landing the most eligible bachelor and closing a bigger, better deal. Not shy about inviting a guy to her place if he hasn't made the first move. Known to wait one night to three dates before closing the deal.

HER CUP OVERFLOWETH

The high altitude in Aspen makes her a cheap drunk and easier to pick up, which explains why men routinely offer to buy drinks right away and try to keep her glass full.

MAGNETS: Attracted to guys with thick wallets and a penchant for ostentatious displays of wealth, status, or power, but any handsome guy with some animal magnetism will do. Occasionally doubles as a *Cougar*.

LISTEN TO THE MONEY TALK

The BBD will size a guy up the minute she meets him. She'll even notice which credit card he uses to pay the bill. (Black AmEx cards are like pheromones.) Regular guys can thwart the investigation and come out on top (if you will), however, by offering mysterious, open-ended answers to probing questions and refocusing the conversation on her. For more on how to add a little mystery, Google "Don Draper's Guide to Picking Up Women."

HABITAT: Tony, members-only Caribou Club; Après-ski hot spot like the Little Nell, Sky, Ajax Tavern, Cache Cache, or Jimmy's; ski slope; high-end store like Gorsuch, Louis Vuitton, Dior, Prada, or Ralph Lauren; expensive local restaurant.

LOCATION: Abundant in Aspen, CO, especially during the holidays. Common to somewhat common in Vail, CO, Sun Valley, ID, and Jackson Hole, WY. Migrates seasonally to and from CA (especially Los Angeles and Orange Counties), New York, South FL, and Las Vegas.

MIGRATION: Frequent flyer.

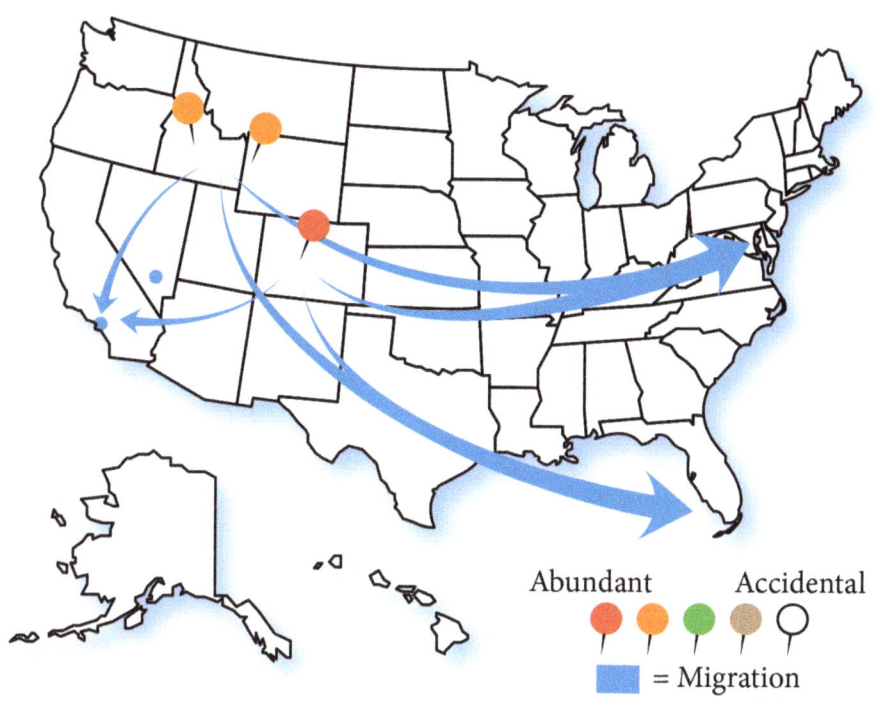

Abundant   Accidental

= Migration

HOLE IN ONE™
(Las Vegas, NV)

APPEARANCE: There are lots of fat women in the buffet lines at Las Vegas casinos, but the Hole in One isn't one of them. She tends to be slender or athletic and toned, with a provocative outfit, plenty of makeup, and a devilish gleam in her eye. Occasionally more average looking, but always dressed to impress and attract attention.

HOLE IN ONE LIGHT

An American woman who resides in Vegas but isn't selling sex (in one way or another) is a "*Hole in One Lite.*" She tends to be much less complicated and more laid-back than the Hole in One, with a casual, Western style; been-there-done-that attitude; and a preference for heavy drinking in local dive bars over the Strip. She also tends to be more relationship-oriented but relatively kinky and/or open-minded about "swinging," threesomes, and other unconventional sexual activities.

HO SPOTTING

A conspicuous minority of Hole in One's are hookers. How can you spot them? If a Hole in One is attractive, scantily clad, and way too easy for an average guy to meet and pick up, chances are she's a ho, especially if she initiates the conversation with him, appears to be alone, and seems a little too familiar with the bar staff. Use your common sense. The Hole in One is promiscuous but rarely a sure-thing unless she's workin' hard for the money.

BEHAVIOR: Amped up and ready to party with a smile and a bounce in her step. Lives for the moment and seeks instant gratification through dancing, drinking, gambling, and sex (with strangers). Also enjoys the shows, concerts, strip clubs and big events, especially on vacation. Often smokes (after a few drinks) or uses recreational drugs.

TRAITS					
Friendliness	😃	😃	😃	😃	
Neuroticism	🗞️	🗞️	🗞️		
Nesting	🥚				
Maintenance	🔨	🔨	🔨		
Superficiality	💰	💰	💰	💰	💰

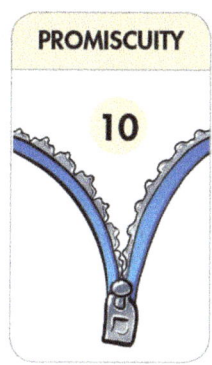

PROMISCUITY: 10

SONG: Common expressions include: "I've never done this before!" "Oh my God!" "Do you have a condom?" and "I'm so fucked up."

MATING: Highly promiscuous and sexually aggressive, even if a guy seems to be taken. Pursues and engages in sexual activity like a man, even if she ordinarily wouldn't act that way someplace else. Normally harmless and carefree but occasionally psycho. Complicated only if a guy cares to see her again after a night or two. Known to wait one night to three "dates" before closing the deal.

SHE HAPPENS IN VEGAS

If you want a one-night stand, lap dance, or some pricey "company," you're in luck. If you're looking for love or a serious relationship, your odds are better at the slot machines.

MAGNETS: Strongly attracted to wealthy men and sugar daddies who subsidize her wild side. Also drawn to boy-toys looking for some action with no strings attached.

HOW MUCH?

Relatively handsome guys with disposable income have what it takes. Their job is to pay for drinks, dinner, drugs, or maybe just an hour of her time.

HABITAT: Hotel/casino; pool party; restaurant; lounge; mall; park; shop; bar or nightclub; strip club.

LOCATION: Abundant in Las Vegas, NV, despite an unfavorable single girl-to-guy ratio, because there are so many women in heat. Common to somewhat common in Portland, OR (with more strip clubs per capita than Las Vegas) and Reno, Lake Tahoe and Laughlin, NV. Somewhat common to casual in Atlantic City, NJ but not nearly as attractive and far more likely to be a ho. Migrates periodically to other cities with an abundance of affluent guys on the prowl, including Miami, New York City, Los Angeles, and Orange County, CA.

MIGRATION: Frequent flyer.

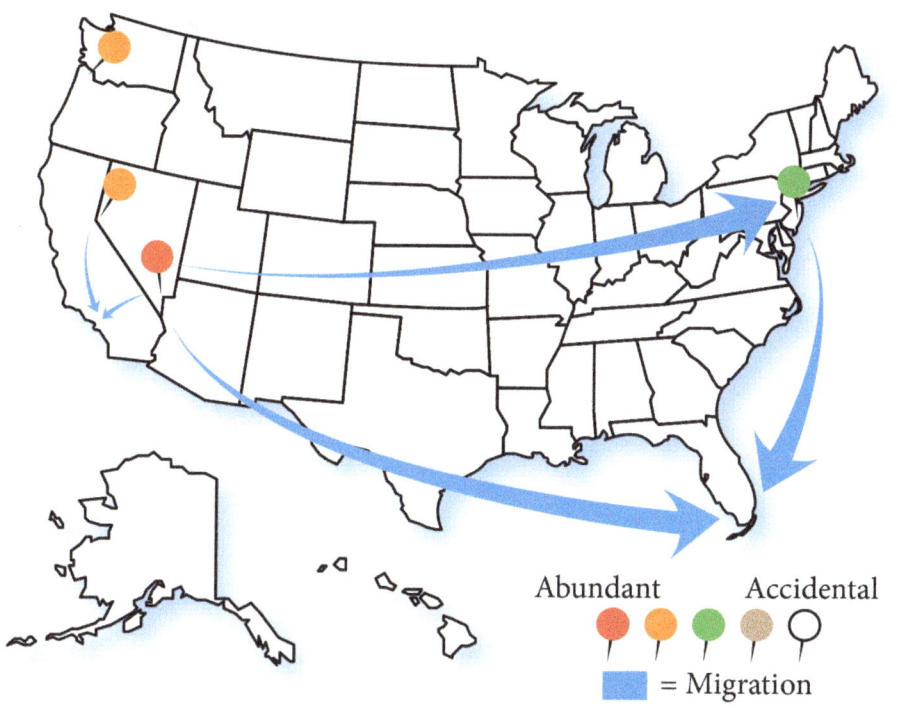

SOUTH BEEOTCH™
(Miami Beach, FL)

120 • WHY LATINAS GET THE GUY

APPEARANCE: (Overly) tan and slender or athletic and toned. Often installs a rack (breast implants) if her boobs aren't naturally big but may not bother if she's already smoking hot or thinks she is. Sunbathes in a skimpy bikini (occasionally topless) and hangs out in oversized designer sunglasses, flip-flops, and as little clothing as possible. Hits the clubs at night in outrageously sexy outfits designed to make men drool.

BEHAVIOR: Lives for the next day at the beach and the party afterwards but not particularly friendly or approachable unless you're on the same program and in her league. Rarely bright, well-educated or religious because it interferes with having a good time. Tends to drink like a fish (at your expense) but dances and exercises so much that it doesn't show. Frequently uses drugs like ecstasy and cocaine to party late into the night and early morning.

TRAITS					
Friendliness	😀	😀			
Neuroticism	🔨	🔨	🔨	🔨	
Nesting	🪺				
Maintenance	🔨	🔨			
Superficiality	💰	💰	💰	💰	💰

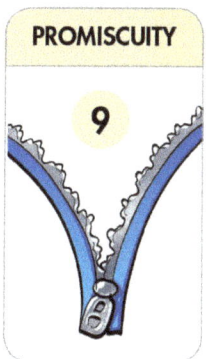

PROMISCUITY 9

SONG: Specializes in the booty call, booty text, and sext. Anything else she has to say in clubs is drowned out by the music, but it hardly matters. It's all small talk. Most of what she wants to say is conveyed in body language.

MATING: Shamelessly promiscuous. Performs an elaborate courtship dance in response to trendy house music. Alcohol and drugs grease the wheels for guys willing to play along, where sex often happens at 4 or 5 a.m. on a weeknight in exchange for the freebies. Often open-minded and enthusiastic about sex with other women — the real deal or just enough to tease men — or multiple partners. Occasionally parties too hard and ends up sloppy drunk, high, or saddled with a venereal disease. Capable of detaching intimacy from sex and "dating" several guys at the same time. Known to wait one night to three "dates" before closing the deal.

IT'S A YOUNG MAN'S GAME

If you're not ready for plenty of sleep deprivation after partying all night (during the week) and overpaying for bottle service in the most exclusive clubs, South Beeotch is not for you.

MAGNETS: Attracted to guys with something to trade for sex, such as VIP treatment at the best clubs and private parties, an impressive boat, fancy car, big house or condo, or free drinks, drugs, and dinners. Good looks go a long way too.

HABITAT: Beach; exclusive nightclub, lounge, or party; Lincoln Road; Bal Harbour Shops; private party; boat or yacht.

LOCATION: Abundant in Miami Beach, FL. Somewhat common in other parts of Miami-Dade County (especially downtown Miami and the Brickell financial district) and Broward County (especially Fort Lauderdale). Occasionally migrates to the Florida Keys, especially wild and heavily-gay Key West.

MIGRATION: Migratory.

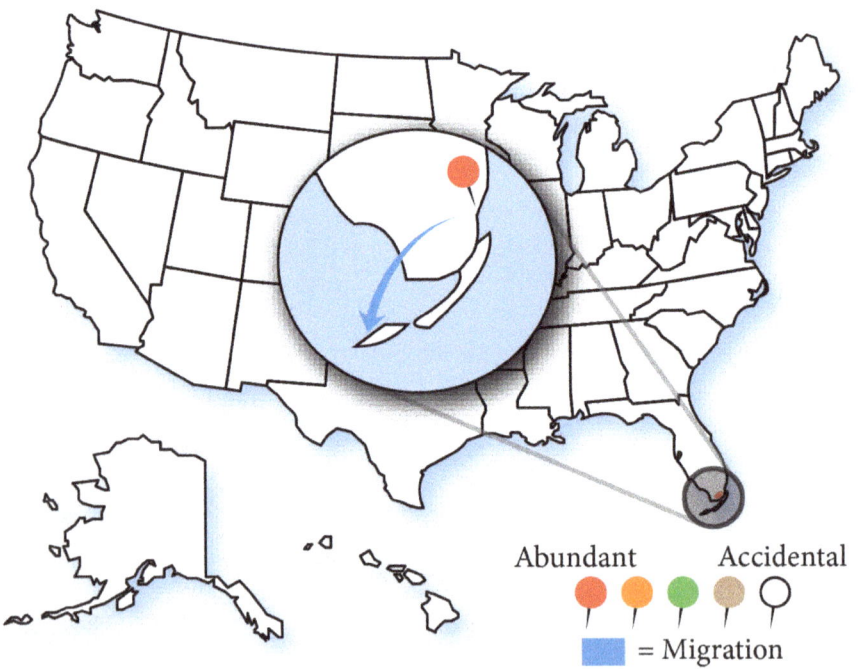

Abundant   Accidental

= Migration

122 • WHY LATINAS GET THE GUY

FREE TRAINING VIDEOS AND TIPS

For free training videos and tips on chickspotting and chicaspotting, visit **JoeBovino.com.**

BOCA BITCH™
(Boca Raton, FL)

APPEARANCE: This borderline-tacky American woman is recognizable by straightened, fried, and highlighted or bottle-blond hair, with extensions; collagen-filled, duck-like lips with extra gloss; long claws with a French manicure; weathered skin with a spray (orangey) tan; large (fake) boobs, and a shapely body sculpted more by nip/tuck than squat/thrust. More average-looking at times. Her night-shift outfit includes high heels, trendy (mostly "True Religion") jeans or a revealing black dress, and a heavy dose of Chanel, Hermes, Louis Vuitton, and Coach merchandise. The day shift calls for plenty of Juicy Couture and big ("Jackie O") sunglasses. Normally in her mid-30s but age varies from 25 to well over 40. Often doubles as a Boca *Cougar*.

BEHAVIOR: Ostensibly wealthy because she married money (and took it in the divorce), gives it up to a rich sponsor (or series of them), or moonlights as a stripper, escort, or hooker. Drives an expensive Benz or Bentley with a big lease even though she doesn't have a real job or any money of her own. A natural-born consumer who lives to shop. Snobbish but usually poorly educated. Frequently lacks class and self-confidence but fakes it reasonably well.

TRAITS					
Friendliness	😊	😃			
Neuroticism	🍾	🍾	🍾		
Nesting	🪺	🪺			
Maintenance	🔨	🔨	🔨	🔨	🔨
Superficiality	💰	💰	💰	💰	💰

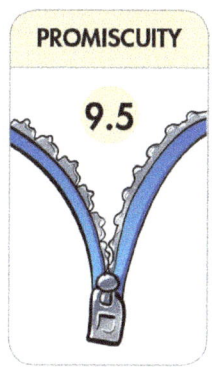

PROMISCUITY 9.5

SONG: Shockingly profane but occasionally funny in a Howard Stern sort of way. Nosy, loudmouthed, and whiny, often with embarrassingly bad manners. Occasionally downright bossy, obnoxious, and rude. Saunters around with an air of insouciance and a dead fish for a handshake. Reapplies lip gloss repeatedly, even at the dinner table. Chomps on gum like a cow chewing its cud. Pauses occasionally for a cigarette.

MATING: Dating, banging, fleecing, and marrying rich men — one after another — is her mission and profession. Anything else she does along the way is a means to that end. Highly competitive, territorial, opportunistic, and suspicious of other women. High-maintenance, relatively untrustworthy, and eager to upgrade. Occasionally preys on young studs for the thrill or other fringe benefits. Known to wait for one or two dates before closing the deal.

CAN'T DANCE, CAN'T SCREW

The Boca Bitch usually has no sense of rhythm on the dance floor. Count on the same performance in bed.

MAGNETS: Attracted to rich men who seem like easy prey. Frequently prefers Jewish guys, but most of them are married or uninterested. As a result, she generally ends up dating flashy, gangsterish "Guido" types and others originally from the Northeast. Non-white men have an excellent shot too as long as they're fully loaded.

BUYER BEWARE

Guys often regret getting involved with the Boca Bitch after she runs off with their shit (in a nasty divorce) or hooks up with another guy (on the side). She means business, fellas. Buyer beware.

HABITAT: Mizner Park; ritzy shopping mall; Neiman Marcus or Saks; Atlantic Avenue in Delray Beach, FL; Boca Raton Resort and Club (by the pool on weekends); high-end restaurant (e.g., New York Prime), bar, or lounge; (day) spa, nail salon, beauty salon, or tanning salon; office of her dermatologist or plastic surgeon.

LOCATION: Abundant in Boca Raton, FL (an otherwise perfectly nice place) but usually a transplant from New York, New Jersey, or eastern Pennsylvania. Also common in nearby Delray Beach, Deerfield Beach, West Palm Beach, Boynton Beach, and Fort Lauderdale. Somewhat common to casual in South Beach. Migrates seasonally between south Florida and cities in the Northeast, Aspen and Vail, CO, and other hangouts of the rich and famous.

MIGRATION: Migratory.

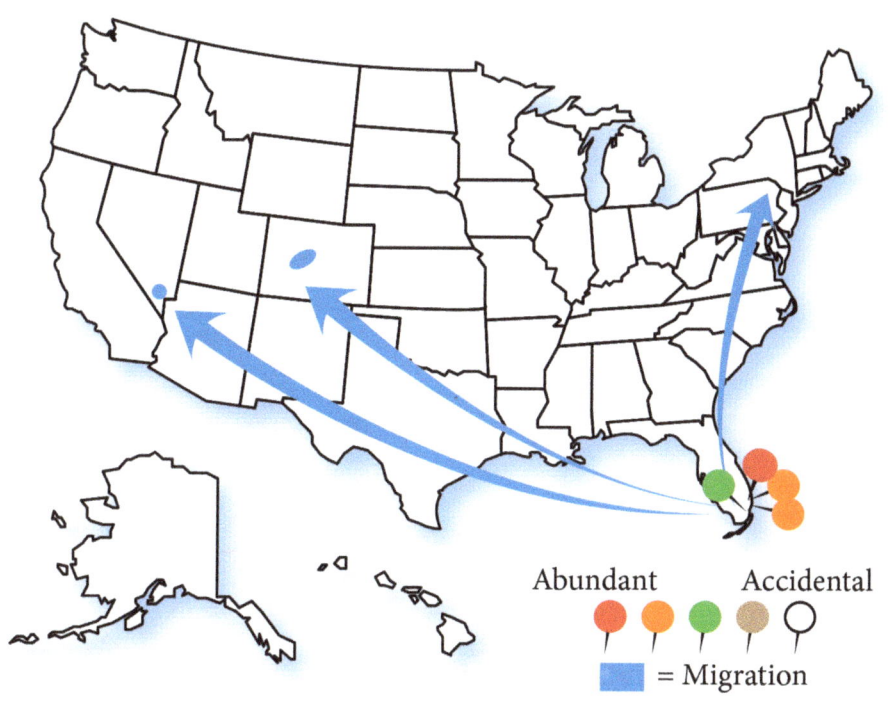

Abundant   Accidental

= Migration

SO HO'™
(New York, NY)

APPEARANCE: This cosmopolitan woman tends to be slender from all the walking around but a bit soft and pale because the weather and fast pace of New York take their toll. Doesn't hesitate to wear unflatteringly casual clothes (e.g., tank top, sweat pants) with little or no makeup for day-to-day errands but tends to be super-trendy, chic, and highly accessorized for work, special events, or a night on the town, with a nice designer jacket and handbag. Occasionally opts for a cooler, more bohemian look if she's artsy, proudly European, or showers less frequently for some other reason. Black is a popular color. Open to cosmetic and plastic surgery — it beats working out and saves time — but not as obsessed with her appearance or the opinions of others as many other American women.

THE SO HO' MO

The So Ho' model (aka the "So Ho' Mo") is notorious for spending hours in front of a mirror to create the illusion that she's gorgeous even when (meticulously) disheveled.

BEHAVIOR: Smart, worldly, and doing just fine without a steady guy (or so she tells herself). Culturally open-minded and tolerant but noticeably cold, jaded, defensive, or bitchy at times, especially around strangers. Often tenacious, intense, and aggressive in pursuit of her goals. Works and plays hard but periodically feels stressed-out and overwhelmed. Tends to be (somewhat) politically liberal or libertarian and relatively non-religious.

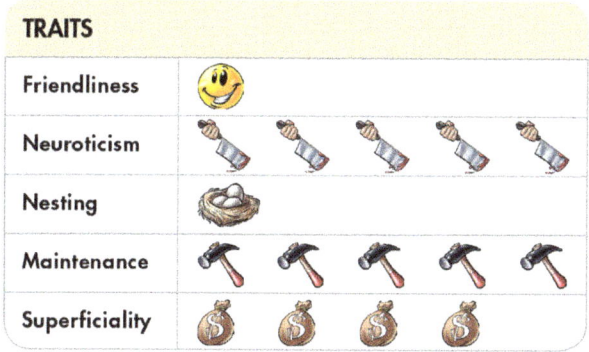
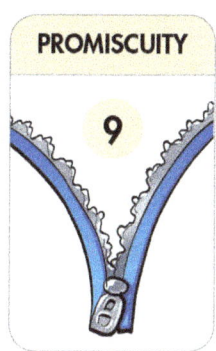

SONG: Highly opinionated, direct, and brutally honest, especially about your shortcomings. Talks loudly and quickly but normally has something (at least marginally) interesting or amusing to say. Often witty and sarcastic, albeit crude, snarky, and condescending at times. Won't hesitate to call you out if you act like a jerk, idiot, racist, or misogynist, which you're bound to do on a regular basis because she redefines those words at will to get her way.

BACK OFF, BUDDY

Maintain a respectful distance from the So Ho' or prepare to be put in your place. This is New York, not Buenos Aires, pal. Don't even think about moving in for a (friendly) kiss on the cheek right off the bat. She doesn't know where your mouth has been and may send it back where it came from.

MATING: Highly promiscuous, fickle, and wary of men in general, as glamorized by the "Sex & The City" television show and movies. Open to the occasional one-night stand or casual fling. Tends to have sex like a man — quickly, detached, or even just to relieve stress — but there's usually a softie (way) behind the tough-chick act. Typically far more concerned about her own needs and pleasure than her partner's, even if she won't admit it. Takes the initiative in courtship and chases the men she really wants, if necessary.

THE THREE-DATE RULE APPLIES

If you're not sleeping with a So Ho' by the end of the third date, she's probably getting it elsewhere. Move on unless you're 99% sure that there's chemistry, she's clearly different from the norm in NYC (e.g., born-again Christian), or she's so hot that you'll willingly accept sloppy seconds.

MAGNETS: Attracted to guys of almost any ethnicity or race who can keep up with her, satisfy her every need, and respect her independence. She wants it all — intelligence, humor, looks, money, and great sex — but usually settles for less because the competition for great guys in New York City is stiff.

HABITAT: City street; restaurant; café; bar; nightclub; Central Park; shopping mall; retail store; art walk or gallery; movie house; theater; acting or comedy class; sporting or cultural event; grocery store; office building; museum.

LOCATION: Abundant in New York City. Common to somewhat common in other parts of New York, South Florida, the East Coast of Florida, and parts of northern New Jersey and Connecticut. Migrates to Aspen and Vail, CO during winter holidays, the Hamptons on New York's Long Island on weekends during the summer, and Florida (especially Miami Beach and Boca Raton) any time of year.

MIGRATION: Frequent flyer.

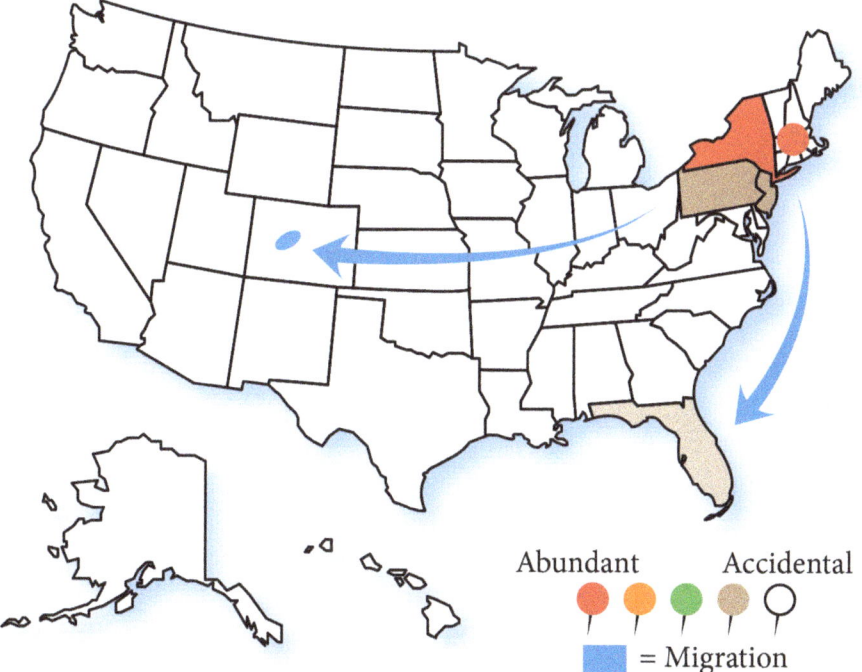

WHY LATINAS GET THE GUY • 131

BRONX TAIL™
(African American – Northeast)

APPEARANCE: Recognizable by her slender but curvaceous bathing-suit-ready ("BSR") figure, featuring a slim waistline; (at least) medium-sized breasts; a high, shapely derriere; full hips; and lean, strong, sexy legs. Occasionally gets a boob job but usually doesn't need it. Often highly fashionable or carefully disheveled and somewhat raw. Sometimes rocks more urban attire, especially in the Bronx and Upper East Side. Regardless of whether she wears long hair extensions, a weave or goes with natural (treated) black or dark brown hair, she *owns* it. Other field marks include: Dark skin, with lighter variations; naturally full lips and strong cheekbones.

BEHAVIOR: Independent and assertive but occasionally cold, neurotic and temperamental. Often highly defensive when wearing a sexy or revealing outfit in order to clearly distinguish herself from a ho. Normally bright and ambitious, especially if she doubles as a *Bougie* (Professional). Rarely uptight but often somewhat traditional and/or religious. Loves to dance, sing and play whenever she can.

TRAITS					
Friendliness	😃	😃			
Neuroticism	💊	💊	💊	💊	💊
Nesting	🪺	🪺	🪺	🪺	
Maintenance	🔨	🔨	🔨	🔨	
Superficiality	💰	💰	💰		

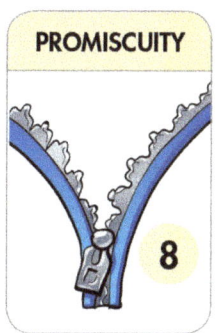

PROMISCUITY 8

SONG: Loquacious, animated and expressive. Laughs freely and frequently. Rather loud unless well-educated. Highly opinionated and sarcastic at times, but less so if *Bougie*.

MATING: Super-territorial, especially in her neighborhood or "borough." Stands by her man in a relationship unless he leaves her alone too long during the cold winter months. Selectively promiscuous otherwise. Relatively high-maintenance. Knows exactly what she's doing and what she wants in the sack. Waits for three dates (more or less) before closing the deal.

MAGNETS: Attracted to handsome, successful black men who know how to treat a lady and seem interested in a genuine relationship. Occasionally dates non-black men who are exceptionally confident, talented, and financially stable.

SURVIVAL OF THE FINEST

Non-black guys have a shot at the Bronx Tail only if they've really got their sh*t together and can handle a strong black chick. Others are in over their heads.

HABITAT: Restaurant, shop, club or bar; office; park; sporting, music, cultural or networking event.

LOCATION: Abundant to common in many parts of the Northeast (where approx. 17.6 % of African Americans live), especially in large cities like Washington, D.C. and New York City, with the largest black urban population in the United States, and a 28% black population in the city overall. Other places with an even higher percentage of Bronx Tails include: Seat Pleasant, Fairmount Heights, Glenarden, Capital Heights, District Heights, Forestville, Forest Heights, Millford Mill, Mitchellville, Lochearn, Temple Hills, and Largo, MD; Lawnside, East Orange, Irvington and Orange, NJ; Blue Hills, CT; and Lakeview, Roosevelt and Wyandanch, NY.

MIGRATION: Migratory.

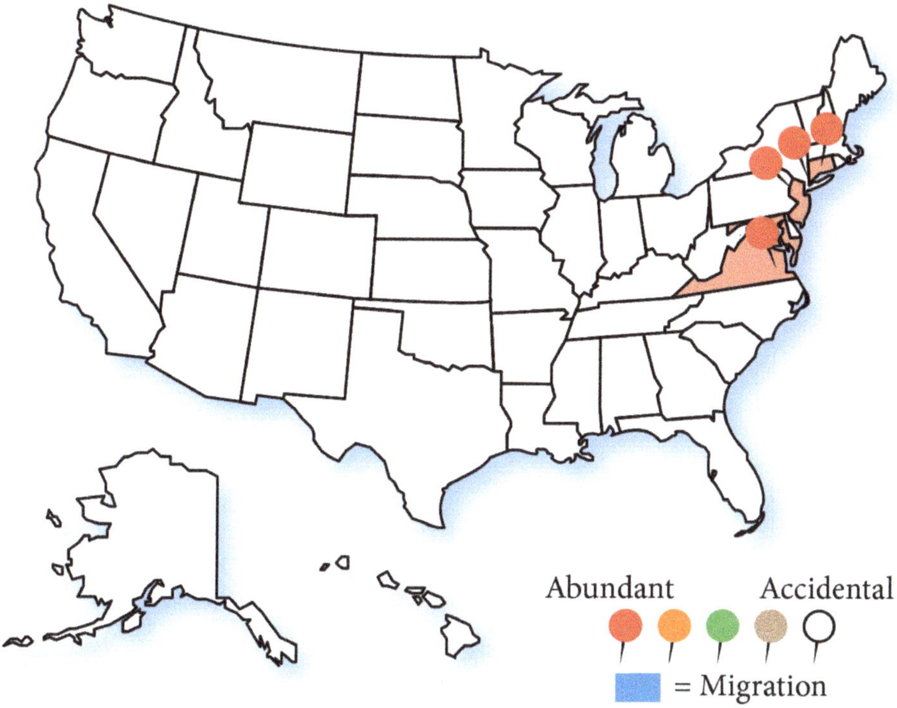

Abundant   Accidental

= Migration

WHY LATINAS GET THE GUY • 135

HURT ROCKER™
(Emo)

APPEARANCE: This emotional, oddly sexy chick, also known as the "Finding Emo," is recognizable by her sour expression; pasty white skin; jet-black short or shoulder-length hair with sharp edges and shapes, usually with (flamboyantly highlighted) bangs covering at least one eye or sections pulled in different directions (and dyed blond at times); thick eyeliner; dark or bright red lips; ridiculously tight jeans; tight, short-sleeved (black or dark colored) T-shirts with the name of her favorite band on them; and beat-up, old-school sneakers. Her (borderline) trashy or slutty outfit also includes (white) studded belts, wristbands and armbands (with bright colors), bright-colored jewelry (with skulls and crossbones), band merchandise, and optional black-rimmed glasses. Piercings are common, especially lip and nipple rings.

EMO, GOTH, OR PUNK?

Try not to confuse the Hurt Rocker with even gloomier Goth chicks or irreverent punk rockers who also tend to wear black clothing and dark makeup on pasty white skin like it's Halloween every day. Hurt Rocker puts a lot of time and energy into her distinctive "emo" style and expects you to notice the difference.

BEHAVIOR: Either suffers from bipolar disorder or acts like she does. Relatively shy, sullen, anti-social, and mysterious, even though she's usually from a comfortable, middle-class family. Tends to avoid eye contact with strangers. Highly sensitive, pessimistic, and cynical. May actually cut her wrists (and cover them with wristbands) if she's really screwed up. Often vegetarian. Loves emo, indie, and underground music; plus "deep" poetry, "art," and taking pictures or video of herself from strange angles to post on Myspace and emo websites.

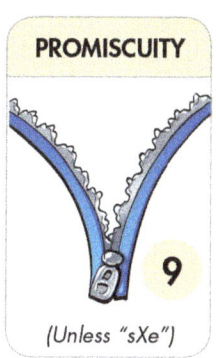

PROMISCUITY

9

(Unless "sXe")

SONG: Vacillates wildly from introverted brooding to emotional outbursts at inappropriate times. Cries and curses frequently.

LET HER VENT

If a guy can't handle a little venting and profanity from the Hurt Rocker, he's not the man for the job. She's going to emote. That's who she is.

MATING: Loves to kiss emo guys, watch emo guys kiss, or kiss another Hurt Rocker. (It's hard to tell them apart.) Typically views sex as a way to boost her poor self-esteem, express her emotions, and feel loved or accepted by others, at least until she matures. Occasionally adopts a "sXe" lifestyle (pronounced "straight edge") and refuses to drink, smoke, masturbate, or have sex. Known to wait one night to three dates before closing the deal (unless sXe).

MAGNETS: Strongly attracted to male emos with similar tastes, interests, and antisocial tendencies. Occasionally dates other guys, especially if they're highly sensitive, emotionally troubled, or there's chemistry for some other reason. Normally avoids posers, jerks, and insensitive players.

LOOKIN' GOOD

It's not easy being (or finding) emo. She spends a lot of time putting on all that makeup, fixing her hair, and selecting the best tight, trashy clothes. So find something pretty and pay her a compliment. She'll almost always appreciate it and may take a liking to you.

HABITAT: Dark emo (dive) bar or club; suburban shopping mall; online (especially MySpace.com, Emocorner.com, Emobucket.com and Vampire Freaks.com).

LOCATION: Common in New Jersey (especially New Brunswick); New York City; Long Island, NY; Washington, D.C.; and Seattle, WA. Somewhat common in the Midwest (especially the suburbs of Chicago and Detroit), the West (especially Los Angeles, San Francisco, and Portland) and other cities with a high mall-to-population density. Casual to accidental elsewhere.

MIGRATION: Somewhat nonmigratory (except in emo circles).

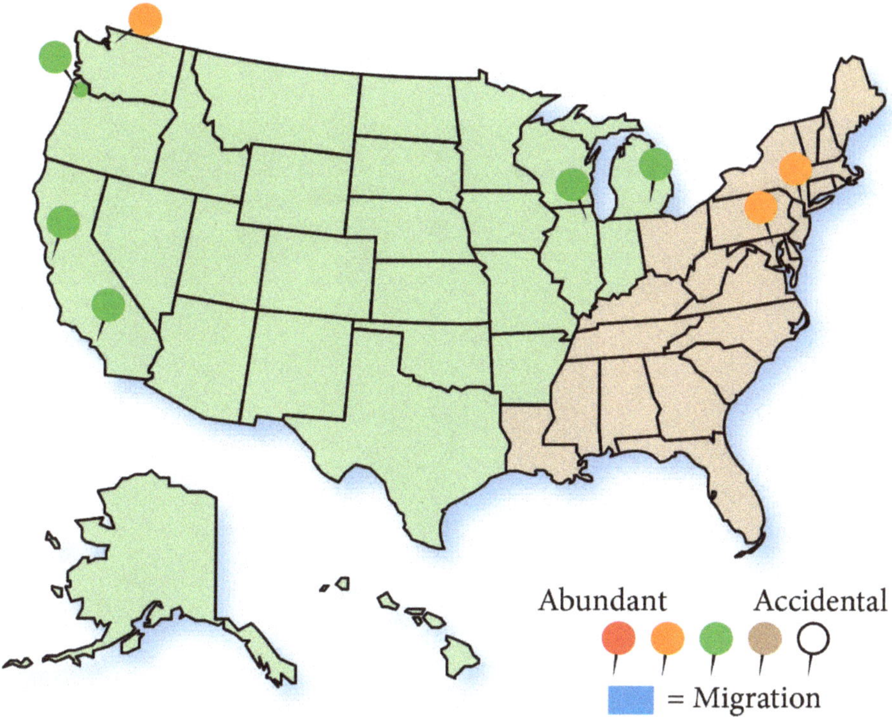

WHY LATINAS GET THE GUY • 139

BROODING BARFLY
(Hipster)

APPEARANCE: This young, slender (but soft), angst-ridden chick, also known as the "PoMo" (Postmodern), strives be unconventionally attractive—with mixed results. Look for tangled, oily (dyed) hair, over-the-top tattoos and piercings, a retro pocketbook, and dark eye bags under sleepy (bloodshot) eyes. Often spotted wearing skinny jeans; wrinkled plaid shirts, vintage tops, and T-shirts; old-school sneakers; a fedora; tie; wristbands; and/or horned-rim or bug-eyed glasses. Rarely wears a bra, heels, makeup, or perfume, and occasionally has hairy and/or musky armpits. Ordinarily pale white but occasionally Asian, nerdy black, or some other ethnic variation.

THE "HAPPY HIPSTER" (PRETTY IN PLAID)

Most American women who dress like a Brooding Barfly aren't the real deal. They're a Happy Hipster™ (also known as the "Bathing Barfly") or some other species who just wants to look cool. How can you tell the difference? If she's happy for an extended period of time, laughs and smiles a lot, and/or doesn't have a conspicuous chip on her shoulder, she's not an authentic, angst-ridden hipster. Modify your approach accordingly.

BEHAVIOR: Bar-hopping malcontent and trend-setting cool-hunter with an obscure taste in clothing, music, literature, and art. Often reasonably well-educated at a liberal arts college. Normally works as a waitress, bartender, barista, hairdresser, or retail clerk (if she's employed at all), but occasionally lands a cool job in the music, art, or fashion industries. Enjoys the late-night hipster bar scene (every day), booze and drugs, body art, reading, kids' games, organic food, smartphones, the Internet, and truly independent music. Seldom religious. Politically liberal.

TRAITS	
Friendliness	😊
Neuroticism	🧂🧂🧂🧂🧂
Nesting	🪺
Maintenance	🔨🔨
Superficiality	💰💰💰💰 (5 if "coolness" counts)

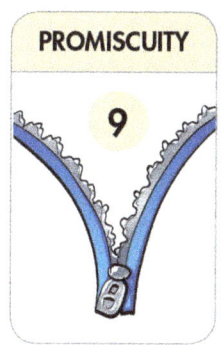

PROMISCUITY 9

TOO COOL FOR ACTING SCHOOL

Don't confuse the Brooding Barfly with the *Mattress* (Los Angeles model/actress). Selling out and sucking up to get famous just isn't cool.

SONG: Frequently expresses smug indifference, disdain, and/or hatred of established social norms (e.g., "work"), institutions (e.g., "Wall Street"), activities (e.g., college football), brands (except Apple), "family values," and tourists. Enjoys talking about herself (if she's in a good mood), witty banter, biting sarcasm, and self-deprecating humor. Curses like a motherf*cker. Known to brag that her vagina is "old school" (natural) and that she liked something "before it was cool."

MATING: Attracts men by acting, talking, dressing, and bathing like she doesn't care what they think. Won't hesitate to approach (hipster) guys or initiate sex, if necessary. Needs a challenge. Rarely goes on a planned "date." Tends to seek drama and instant gratification rather than love or lasting friendship, but shit happens. Known to wait one night to two months before closing the deal.

MAGNETS: Strongly attracted to narcissistic hipster guys, especially tall, skinny, pasty white ones with a bad attitude. Occasionally dates mysterious non-hipster men. Interracial dating is common.

HABITAT: Dive bar, lounge, or hipster party/dance club; independent bookstore, art gallery, music venue, movie house, theater, or free outdoor event; local coffee shop; park; marijuana store; poetry reading; Apple store; Goodwill; Salvation Army; flea market; thrift store; subway station.

LOCATION: Abundant to somewhat common in urban settings, including Brooklyn (especially Williamsburg); Manhattan (Lower East Side); Chicago (Wicker Park); Seattle (Capitol Hill); Richmond (The Fan); Philadelphia (Old City and Fishtown); Austin, TX (East Austin); Minneapolis (Whittier); Los Angeles (Echo Park and Silver Lake); Washington, DC (U Street); Boston (Jamaica Plain); San Francisco (Inner Mission, see **49er**); Detroit (Hamtramck); Baltimore (Mt. Vernon, Fells Point); Atlanta (Little Five Points and Cabbagetown); Milwaukee (Riverwest); Cleveland (Coventry and Tremont); and New Orleans (Lower Garden District).

MIGRATION: Frequent flyer.

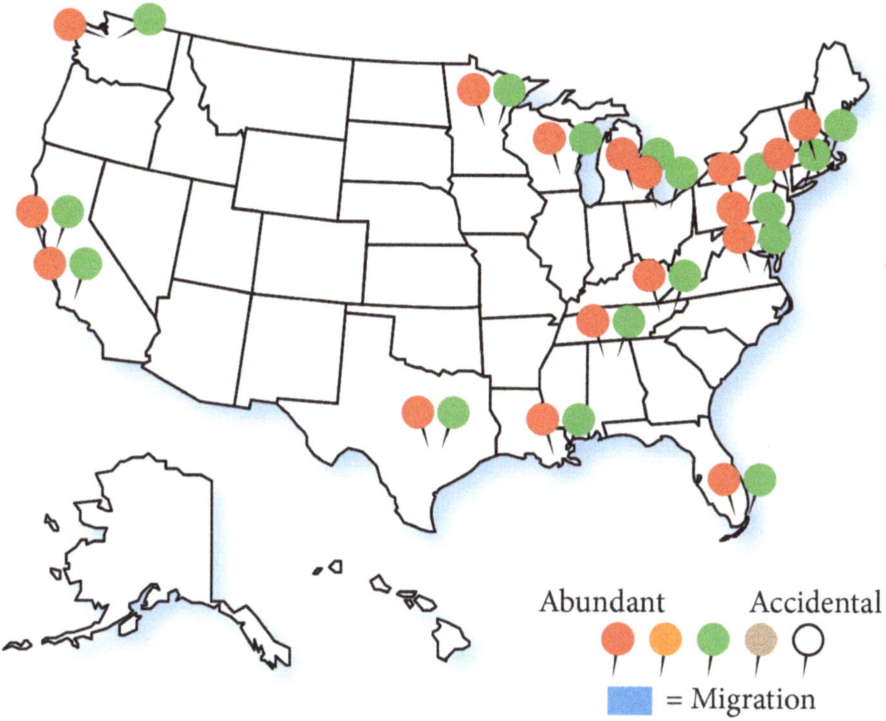

WHY LATINAS GET THE GUY • 143

BIG BANG™
(Rubenesque)

APPEARANCE: This easily identifiable American chick, also known as the Big Beautiful Woman ("BBW"), is exceptionally fat or obese. Other common field marks include cherubic cheeks; full lips; a big, round body; flabby upper arms; large, pendulous breasts; and a plump, extra-large booty.

FREE TO BE FAT

Despite her excess weight, the Big Bang enjoys food and often considers it a perk of being big. Unlike women who gain weight temporarily during a pregnancy or after an illness, the Big Bang tends to stay that way unless she gets a stomach staple or a really, really good diet plan.

SONG: Frequently chats about her (losing) battle of the bulge, fatty foods, and related health problems, but normally doesn't take herself too seriously. Commonly opines that other women (with perfect bodies) are "too skinny" or "fake."

THE BIG BANG THEORY

If you want to date or foster harmony with a Big Bang, don't talk about her weight. If you can't avoid the subject, use positive words like "curvy," "voluptuous," "BBW," or "full-bodied." Avoid loaded ones like "fat," "overweight," "obese," and "Her Thighness" in any non-clinical setting. And think twice before referring to her as "chubby," "plump," "plus-sized," or even "Rubenesque." You're walking on thin ice — hopefully solo.

BEHAVIOR: Omnivorous. Inclined to indulge her appetite for fast food, fried food, ice cream — including Ben & Jerry's aptly named "Chubby Hubby" flavor — and oversized portions of everything else. Often relatively friendly to strangers of both sexes but somewhat insecure and highly sensitive about her weight. Tends to be less affluent than average because the top 10 fattest states largely overlap with the top 10 poorest ones.

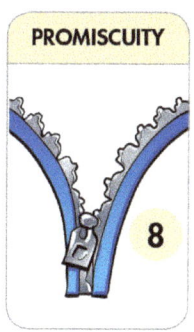

MATING: Normally a bit shy or hesitant about intimacy but opens up (relatively) quickly to men with a sincere interest in a meaningful relationship or clear preference for big women. Known to wait for up to three dates before closing the deal.

MAGNETS: Attracted to guys who think she's sexy and attractive just as she is. Tends to appreciate non-superficial strengths in men, including a keen sense of humor — goofiness and wit go over better than wisecracks or teasing — amiability, intelligence, and a genuine love for kids and family.

MORE TO LOVE

Americans often equate beauty with thinness and stigmatize chubbiness, but beauty is in the eye of the beholder and some men prefer a Big Bang to skinny women.

BREAKING RACIAL BARRIERS ONE BIG BANG AT A TIME

The white Big Bang is more likely to enter into an inter-racial relationship than thinner white women in America, presumably because a disproportionately large number of black, Latin, and Middle Eastern men appreciate her extra pounds and big booty.

HABITAT: (Fast food) restaurant; all-you-can-eat joint; warehouse store; casino (buffet line); hippocampus; ice cream or pizza parlor.

LOCATION: Finding a Big Bang in the American field is a piece of cake, if you will. Approximately two-thirds of American adults are technically overweight or obese. According to CalorieLab's "United States of Obesity 2014" study and map, Mississippi led the fat pack for the 6th straight year (35.1% obese in 2013 and 69.3% obese or overweight in 2013), followed closely by West Virginia, Louisiana, Arkansas, Alabama, Oklahoma, Kentucky, South Carolina, Michigan, Indiana, and Tennessee. Colorado is the leanest state, but the Big Bang is common there too.

MIGRATION: Somewhat nonmigratory (but varies regionally).

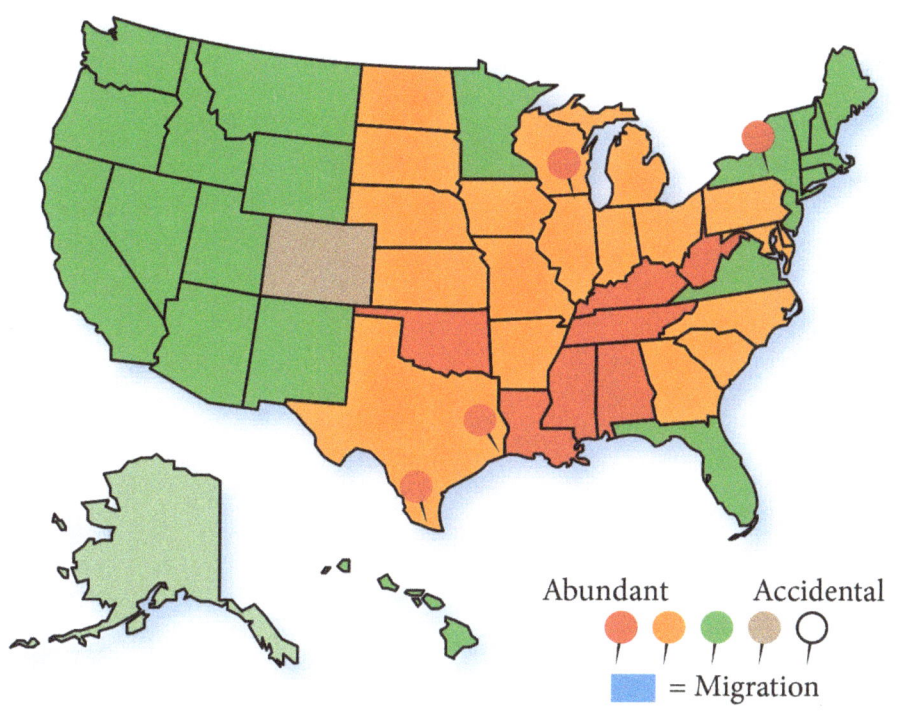

WHY LATINAS GET THE GUY • 147

COUGAR
(Sexual Predator)

APPEARANCE: This frisky American chick in her sexual prime (35 to 50 years old) can still turn heads. Often wears tight (loud) clothing with a padded bra, visible cleavage, lots of bling, and f*ck-me pumps. Doesn't have the hard body she had in her late 20s or early 30s but stays relatively fit to attract younger men. Uses tanning, (heavy) makeup, good grooming, cosmetic wizardry, and plastic surgery — especially optional breast implants for sagging boobs — to maintain the illusion of youth. Occasionally goes way overboard.

THE COUGAR FAMILY

Other members of the Cougar family include the "Puma" (under 35) and the "Sabertooth," "Snow Leopard," or "Mountain Goat" (over 50, menopause, dentures).

BEHAVIOR: A seasoned MILF, divorcee, widow, or childless career-oriented woman on the biological clock. Tends to be smart, financially successful (one way or another), and goal-oriented. Ostensibly confident (in some ways), dominant, and determined to get her way. Occasionally jaded and cynical about men, especially older ones.

TRAITS	
Friendliness	😊 😊 😊
Neuroticism	🍾 🍾 🍾
Nesting	🪺 🪺
Maintenance	🔨
Superficiality	💰 💰 💰 💰

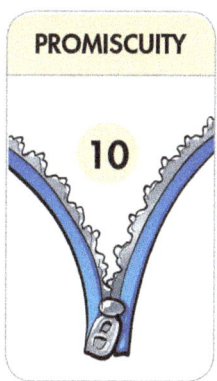

PROMISCUITY: 10

SONG: Doesn't hesitate to talk dirty, in or out of bed, or cut to the chase. Lies about her age if necessary.

MATING: A stalk-and-ambush predator who preys on much younger men. Sly, smooth, seductive, and cunning as she goes for the kill. Often prefers to be the aggressor and enjoys role reversal. Non-committal as she moves from one younger mate to the next. Usually has a been-there-done-that attitude toward marriage. Rarely plays the head games that younger American women do and knows exactly what she's doing in bed. Closes the deal early and often ... if she can.

HOT FOR TEACHER

She may be a little old and wrinkly, and her relationships with younger men may have no long-term potential whatsoever, but she's a seasoned slut who can teach her disposable boy-toys a thing or two in and out of the bedroom.

MAGNETS: Attracted to guys in their 20s or early 30s with no beer belly, a full head of hair, and an overactive libido to match her own. Expands the net in her 40s and 50s to include men in their mid to late 30s.

HABITAT: Cougar "den" (posh lounge or bar teeming with Cougars); dating or social networking website; beauty salon; café; grocery store; athletic club; yoga studio; local fair or carnival; high-end boutique, restaurant, or shopping center.

LOCATION: Abundant to common in Orange and Los Angeles Counties, CA; San Diego and San Francisco, CA; Aspen and Boulder, Colorado; Boca Raton, Orlando, and West Palm Beach, FL; Las Vegas, NV; New York City; Nashville, TN; and Austin, TX. Somewhat common to casual in many other places, especially large metropolitan areas on the East and West Coasts.

MIGRATION: Migratory.

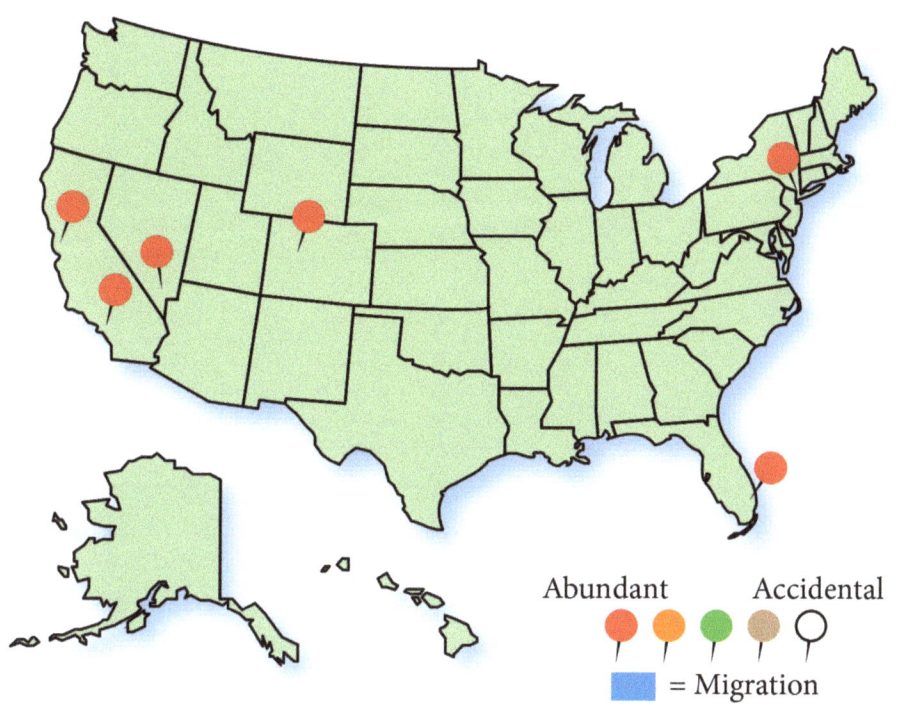

WHY LATINAS GET THE GUY • 151

YOU'RE ALMOST THERE!

Chuck Yeager was the first person to break the sound barrier. Here's what he said:

"At the moment of truth, there are either reasons (excuses) or results."

Are you ready to take your dating and relationships to the next level?
Visit **JoeBovino.com**.

CHAPTER FIVE

THE GHOST TO GODDESS PRINCIPLES

"If you do what you've always done, you'll get what you've always gotten."

— Tony Robbins

How to Go from Ghost to Goddess

As noted in the Introduction of this book, many American women struggle with dating and relationships in today's hook-up culture, feeling unattractive, undesirable or even invisible when Latinas and other sexy, confidently feminine women run off with the best guys.

It's not a pretty sight, but there's still plenty of time for a comeback.

The secret is to empower American women by making it cool to be nice, respectful, friendly, family-oriented, and *feminine* again, while retaining and strengthening the competitive advantages that so many American women already enjoy (e.g., decency, intelligence, sense of humor, fluency in English, financial independence).

America needs a lot more women like that.

Once again, I'm not advocating weakness. Femininity equals weakness only in the minds of unattractive women with an attitude problem.

Think of it this way: Do Sophia Vergara, Shakira, Jennifer Lopez, and Eva Longoria seem like *weak* women to you? Ugh, no. I don't think so.

The following 10 *Ghost to Goddess* Principles are designed to help American women turn the heads and win the hearts of America's most eligible bachelors (again) by being the best they can be.

I hope they make a difference for you and would love to hear from you if they do.

Principle #1: Say "Thank You" Every Day

You can't improve your life or your luck with men until you improve your attitude. It all starts on the inside. Good things rarely happen to miscreants and malcontents who walk around looking at their shoes with a frown on their face, a chip on their shoulder, and a snide comment on the tip of their tongue. Visualize Kara Brown of Jezebel at a flea market. Ugh.

So, before you do anything else, take a few minutes each day to count your blessings. Say "*Thank you*" to Jesus, God, your "Higher Power," your best friend, or the dog — whatever works for you. You can even thank me, if you want to. (Just kidding! I prefer expensive gifts.) I don't care who you thank for your blessings, but I strongly recommend that you take time to thank someone or something besides yourself.

Then, ask for a little divine guidance to act on your beliefs and dreams, whatever they are. If you don't know what to do or say, try this simple prayer: "*Show me the way.*" Then, don't just sit there. Get going! Works every time.

I know this Principle may sound corny or cliche to some of you, but there are many studies demonstrating that the key to happiness, peace of mind, and many other good things in life, is *gratitude*.

Yoga, meditation and other relaxing activities are good for you, but there's no substitute for putting your problems aside briefly each day and thanking God or someone besides yourself for the blessings in your life, including things that most of us take for granted, like our individual liberties, health, loving family members, and old friends. I don't know you, but I know this: If you're alive and kicking, you have plenty to be grateful for — especially if you were lucky enough to be born in the United States — and there's nothing worse than an ingrate. Well, maybe a bitchy ingrate.

Besides the benefits of just being a happier person for the rest of your life who's more prepared to answer the door when opportunity knocks, you'll be instantly more attractive to good men, and more desirable as a potential partner. Men love happy women, particularly when they're happy for reasons having nothing to do with the relationship. Why? Besides the obvious benefits of hanging around a cheerful person, men don't feel pressure to *make* you happy. Only *you* can make yourself happy for any extended period of time. All men can do is try to improve your life by being there for support, companionship, and unconditional love when it counts.

Consider the Brazilian American *Bumbshell*, for example. She's arguably the most promiscuous of America's Latinas, which can be problematic for guys. She's also known to be fickle and less than completely honest at times. But guys routinely overlook these drawbacks because the Bumbshell also tends to be grateful for the simplest of blessings, habitually happy, "thumbs-up" positive, and non-confrontational. It's adorable, even when she says "Não."

She's the anti-bitch.

Principle #2: Keep It Simple, Stupid!

No, I'm not calling you "Stupid." I'm advising you to apply the Keep It Simple, Stupid ("KISS") principle to men, dating and relationships from now on.

There's nothing worse than filling your mind with mush — in other words, reading Jezebel, Huff Post Women, or *Why Men Love Bitches* — when you're trying to make meaningful, positive changes in your life. It inevitably leads to confusion, frustration, costly mistakes, and failure.

There's no need to redefine words, ignore facts, delude yourself, act like somebody you're not (a bitch, a man), or make excuses for men who don't cut the mustard. The raw, unfiltered truth is usually right there in front of us. It's simple and manageable.

Let's stick with that, shall we? Yes, we can!

Principle #3: Treat Him Better Than Rodney Dangerfield

Rodney Dangerfield is known for the catchphrase "I don't get no respect!" and his comedic monologues on that theme. He was hilarious, but most men who say that to you or about you won't stick around if they have a choice.

If you disrespect, dislike or hate men, and it's reflected in the things you say and do, *nothing else matters*. You can do everything else right and still lose a great guy if you emasculate him for any extended period of time. He doesn't need you in his life to do that. The Internet, sitcoms, women's talk shows, movies, and the American court system already do it on a daily basis. You're supposed to make his life *better*.

Men want and need to feel important, valued, and respected in a relationship. It's in our DNA. So, if you've got a good man, do and say little things to make him feel that way any chance you get. That's not asking too much, is it? If he doesn't feel like a man, he won't act like one, and there's a Latina around the corner who'd be more than happy to step in and rectify the situation.

To be fair, I acknowledge that a tiny minority of men get off on being treated like sh*t, at least once in a while. I have two friends in Los Angeles who worked part-time as dominatrices several years ago. (No, I was never a client. Relax.) Each told me shocking stories about guys who'd come to them for verbal and, to a much lesser extent, physical abuse. (One gal did the whole thing over the Skype. "Fix your tutu! Now, dance around like a ballerina! You're a loser! You'll never get a girl like me!" "You're disgusting!" Unbelievable.) Apparently, at least 80% of their clients were wealthy (mostly Jewish) men who were masters of their domain at the office. Go figure.

There are definitely a few oddballs out there, but most guys want absolutely no part of this dominatrix crap. They want to be loved and respected, and there's no f*cking way they'd ever wear a tutu.

Principle #4: Retain and Strengthen Your Competitive Advantages

American women have some competitive advantages when it comes to attracting, getting and keeping a great American guy, even if a sexy Latina has her eye on him. These should be retained, strengthened and leveraged as much as possible.

For one thing, fully assimilated American women are American citizens who speak English fluently and share many useful cultural references with American men (e.g., TV shows, movies, and politics). Many American women are also well-educated and financially independent and/or come from close-knit families. Americans are also generally known for their ready sense of humor — English is a playful language — and a certain appreciation of what's "cool." That's not a complete list, but you get the idea.

I've heard that words like "compete," "competition," "market" and "dating market" rub most American women the wrong way because they don't want to compete for men and don't think they need to. They expect to just show up and get whatever they want from men, like Reannon Muth in Japan. Some, like the author of *Why Men Love Bitches*, go so far as to say it's "demeaning" to compare yourself to other women or compete against them for the best guys. You should tell men to "Take it or leave it!"

That's nonsense. Like it or not, we all live in the real world where people compete for things, including love and affection from non-family members. And it's *OK*. There's no need to obsess over the competition or waste time worrying about not being good enough to win.

Instead, take action. Study the strengths and weaknesses of your competition. Consider how you match-up and what you can do to improve your odds of success in the field. Then simply *execute your game plan and give your best effort*. If it works for Bill Belichick and Tom Brady of the New England

Patriots — and every other successful sports team for that matter — it can work for you. No biggie. Enjoy the game of life.

By the way, funny and snarky aren't the same thing. Being funny is an asset that can help you on the road from ghost to goddess. Snarkiness, on the other hand — that is, having a rudely critical tone or manner — is a liability. Militant feminists are habitually snarky. Their blog posts typically drip of bitterness and contempt. Get your humor someplace else.

Principle #5: Copy That

Tony Robbins knows a thing or two about motivating people to improve their lives, and he's right about a fundamental, overarching principle for achieving success in getting the guy: "*To be successful (in getting the guy), find someone who's achieved the results you want and copy what they do.*"

Think about it. Have "Alpha Bitch" Gigi Engle, Kara Brown (Jezebel's resident flea-market shrew) or any other militant feminist really achieved the results you want with men? No, unless you define success as making yourself repugnant. Latinas, on the other hand, are succeeding with men in ways that can work for you right away — bass or no bass — if you copy what they do.

Not everything they do. Just the stuff that works.

Look (More) Like a Latina

Latinas often go to extraordinary lengths to look like a million bucks every time they leave the house, and men *love* it. They look pretty damn good inside the house too, come to think of it. This is particularly evident in Miami and other parts of South Florida, but not only there.

They do it because it makes them happy to look sexy and feminine, not out of weakness, and they enjoy doing things that please men. They feel more confident and empowered as a woman when they look beautiful. Consequently, with some exceptions, Latinas normally attend meticulously to their hair, makeup, clothing, and accessories; proudly show off their best assets, even if they're overweight; and take advantage of cosmetic and plastic surgery, if necessary. Most (non-Mexican) Latinas workout regularly, too.

American women often look like slobs or pseudo-men by comparison. Just look at the contrast between a San Francisco *49er* or Seattle

Perfect 6, on the one hand, and a *Euro-Mina* (Argentine American) or *La Guitarra* (Puerto Rican – South) on the other. Then there's the American *Big Bang* (Rubenesque woman), who's easy to spot in all 50 States.

Guys are visual. We may be simple, but we're not stupid, and we have a choice.

So step it up, ladies. Not all of you. You know who you are. Study the Latinas, especially the ones you admire the most. Watch them, listen carefully to what they say, and *copy* what they do to look that good on a regular basis. You don't need a Latin booty to be gorgeous, and you know it. Some men don't even like a big butt. Just do the best you can with what God gave you.

Supermodel-hot women can get away with baggy sweatpants, oversized t-shirts, bad hair, no shower, and no makeup in public. The rest of you can't, especially if you don't have a great body. Latinas rarely let their guard down and run around town looking like that. You shouldn't either.

Many Latinas even manage to look sexy at the gym, by the way, which is why I put the *Symmetrical Force* on an elliptical trainer in her profile. I've seen it in person many times. It's … motivating.

Act (More) Like a Latina

- *Turbocharge Your Natural, God-Given Femininity*

By and large, Latinas *like* being womanly, sexy, seductive, and highly feminine. It comes naturally, and they're not interested in faking it. It doesn't matter whether they're poor and financially dependent or wealthy and well-educated with a successful career of their own. Either way, *they don't want to be masculine or act like men*. They expect *real* men to do that. I know … What a concept!

Needless to say, guys love it. You can find exceptions to the rule who seemingly prefer their women to wear the pants in a relationship, but do you really want to carry some loser's balls around in your purse all day?

Some American women get it, particularly in Texas, other Southern States and parts of the Midwest. They don't need anyone to tell them to be feminine.

Many Asian, Middle Eastern and European women also view femininity in a more positive light than American ones. They get the guy, too.

One of them, British-Lebanese Amal Alamuddin, even convinced George Clooney to tie the knot. Another, Chinese-Vietnamese-American Priscilla Chan, wed billionaire Facebook CEO Mark Zuckerberg. I don't know either woman, but Lebanese-American women (90% of whom are Christian) "tend to be feminine but rarely a feminist" and "loyal to [their] huge, well-connected family, especially the elders," to quote my first book. Likewise, Chinese-American women tend to be "independent but family-oriented and raised to nurture and please [their] man." Men like these things.

Not surprisingly, American feminists have tried to spin all of this to their advantage. One blogger for Huff Post Women, Kristen Houghton, actually claims that these high-profile celebrity marriages changed the meaning of "trophy wife." Before Clooney and Zuckerberg tied the knot, American men preferred a "docile" woman who would act as a "servant" and "brainless beauty on [their] arm at social functions …" But now, "[b]rains are the new beauty." Miraculously, "the most attractive and sexually desirable women" are "alpha" bitches who aren't "afraid to *intimidate* any male that has antiquated ideas of gender roles." (my italics) We should rejoice in the "rise of the alpha woman" and exclaim "Hooray equality!"

Not so fast.

Ms. Houghton's article is misleading for three reasons. First, George Clooney married a *foreigner* and Zuckerberg married a woman who, while born in the United States, appears to identify with Chinese culture and/or Confucianism. Neither one fits the description of a fully assimilated, non-hyphenated "American woman" in this book. Second, if brains are the new beauty and looks aren't that important anymore, why did Clooney, in particular, choose to marry such a hottie? Third, Ms. Houghton and her ilk are so obsessed with being "strong," gaining "power," and becoming "alpha" that they undermine more important and appealing feminine qualities.

What should you do to tap into your natural, God-given femininity?

First, change your mindset. Stop equating femininity with weakness — it's apples and oranges — and stop confusing the legitimate quest for equal justice under the law and success in the workplace with a counterproductive quest for equality with men in *all* things. Men and women are genetically different. (I realize that the distinction may not be obvious in Seattle and San Francisco, but trust me on this one). We're not exactly the same and never will be. Accept it and focus instead on being the best, non-bitchy *woman* you can be. Everything else will work itself out.

Second, look for ways that Latinas express their femininity and allow their men to be masculine. Then copy some of those behaviors and incorporate them into your routine until they become second-nature. Most of them are simple courtesies, little things that you'd do without thinking if you weren't so busy trying to be masculine. I'm not going to use this space for a laundry list of examples, and I shouldn't have to. You know what to do, and if you're not sure, watch the Latinas.

Be sure to notice what Latinas *don't* do as well because eliminating ugly "Alpha Bitch" behaviors can be as important as adding some more feminine ones. Soon, you'll be a fully loaded, confident, highly feminine, American Goddess ... whether or not you choose to spend part of your day in a boardroom. It's not a zero-sum game.

Third, learn to flirt like a lady. Flirtatiousness is a Southern tradition, but American women in many parts of the country apparently didn't get the memo. That's unfortunate because men love women who can flirt. Dating site winks and social media pokes aren't the same. Anyone can do that.

Most Latinas also flirt like pros. They do it in a cute, sexy, welcoming way that makes a man want to approach, even if he's normally shy. (They're not likely to do his job for him, however.) This kind of flirting is hard to resist and — for most single guys — can't happen often enough.

So, watch how Latinas and Southern women flirt (in person or via YouTube) and identify a few simple moves that might work for you. Read some books or articles on the subject, too. I just Googled "flirting" and found "*11 Pretty Cool Things You Didn't Know About Flirting,*" for example. Not bad.

Then take some chances out there. And don't worry! I can't think of a single occasion *in my entire life* when a woman flirted with me, successfully or unsuccessfully, and I wasn't flattered.

- *Welcome and Appreciate Attention from Men (Be Nice for Goodness' Sake!)*

Latinas aren't always easy to meet, but they're generally more approachable, sociable and friendly than their American counterparts, especially outside of the Southern States. The only Latina subculture profiled in Chapter Three that didn't rank at least average (2 ½ smiley faces) for friendliness was the *Nuyorican* (Puerto Rican–Northeast), but that's largely attributable to extensive intermingling of Latin and black cultures in the region. Her Puerto Rican counterpart in Florida, *La Guitarra,* ranks much higher.

Men don't like women who go through life with a hostile, defensive, standoffish attitude, as if they're too good to talk with or even acknowledge anyone around them. As noted in Chapter One, Jezebel's Kara Brown went off on some poor guy at a flea market in Los Angeles because he had the audacity to give her a compliment in public. Unfortunately, Ms. Brown isn't unique. I've seen this kind of rudeness from American women many times, in various forms. Men notice it, and we don't find it remotely appealing.

In contrast, Latinas generally seek out, expect and *welcom*e attention from men when they go out, even if the attention has (God forbid!) sexual overtones. They appreciate compliments too, as noted in the *Cinnamon Swirl* profile, for example. There's no way a *Cinnamon Swirl* unleashes an bitter tirade like Jezebel's Kara Brown when some guy walks up and says "Hey, Beautiful" at a flea market. No way.

Even celebrity Latinas tend to be nicer than American ones. One of my American buddies was at an airport a few years ago when Shakira arrived with her entourage. Since he was a fan, he walked up to her at the Baggage Claim and said something, even though he normally wouldn't do such a thing. Most American female celebrities would have given him a half-smile, a barely audible "thank you" and either quickly turned away or signaled for a bodyguard to intervene. Not Shakira. The conversation didn't last long, but she was extremely friendly and down-to-earth the whole time, as if her celebrity status was no big deal and she appreciated her fans. My friend was delighted and couldn't get over how nice she was. He will never forget it.

Men love it when a woman is confident and comfortable enough in her own skin to appreciate and welcome attention from men who find her attractive, and secure enough to know that they can handle him if he steps over the line. Latinas score big points here.

That's why you should copy the Latinas by being friendlier, more approachable, and more welcoming to men, as long as they keep a respectful distance. I know it's not easy to deal with strangers who call out or approach you sometimes, but try to handle it in stride, preferably with a *smile*.

You never know who might walk up next.

- *Place a Higher Priority on Family*

Latinas almost always place family at the top of their priority list. In fact, in 13 of the 14 profiles in Chapter Three, the Latina scored at least a 4 (out of 5) for Nesting, and the only remaining one (*Nuyorican*) scored 3 ½. Men love it, even if they're not particularly family-oriented themselves, because women who believe strongly in family and traditional family values are more likely to treat them lovingly and respectfully in a relationship and raise happy, well-balanced children. They're also less likely to cheat, file for a divorce, or run off with the kids and half of the family's assets.

Many American women bristle at the suggestion that they should be more loyal and family-oriented. Some object because they had a lousy upbringing themselves. Others think "family-oriented" and "family values" are code words for losing their independence, career, or "reproductive rights" to become stay-at-home moms. Well, I'm not using code words in this book and don't see it that way.

Believe it or not, most men like it when a woman has a career of her own or something else that she's passionate about besides them. It makes her more interesting and sexy, and the extra money generated (if any) can make it easier to live larger or travel more together. However, if a woman's career overshadows her family life to the point where it's obvious that she could take it or leave it, men start to wonder about whether it makes sense to become the newest member of a dysfunctional family.

You may also be surprised to hear that a significant percentage of America's Latinas are relatively well-educated, entrepreneurial and/or successful in a career of some kind, especially in cities like Miami. I've met many gorgeous Venezuelan-American *Trifectas* with advanced degrees in engineering, IT, business, and law, for example, even though they could've gotten by solely on their looks. And yes, every one of them was family-oriented. In fact, it's hard to find a Latina who *isn't* family-oriented, even if she's single and pursuing a promising career. They exist, especially among the younger, more fully assimilated generation, but they're rare.

Many American women utter the right clichés about the importance of family but screw their men anyway. It's as if the concept of "family" doesn't necessarily include the man, especially after a kid or two, when he's served his purpose and can henceforth be replaced, ignored or fleeced in court. I know that most of you aren't like this, but it happens often enough these days to make (American) guys seriously question the true importance of family — or, more specifically, a husband — to American women. Some men boycott American women altogether because of this. It's a big, bright red flag.

What should you do? Copy the Latinas. Talk is cheap. Instead, behave as if family matters and there's an important role for a good man to play in yours, even if you're a busy career woman. Show him that your concept of family doesn't revolve solely around kids and parents or grandparents. You understand the importance of a great boyfriend and husband, too. Guys pick up on this stuff, and it greatly affects the choices they make about who to date and marry, and who to leave behind.

Have Sex (More) Like a Latina

Latinas may dress provocatively and look sexy most of the time, but — with a few exceptions — they aren't as slutty or promiscuous as American women, and it works to their advantage with men.

There are regional and cultural variations, of course, but America's Latinas tend to make guys wait *at least* a month before sex, especially in Miami, and they give guys plenty of rope to hang themselves in the interim. Even the Brazilian American *Bumbshell*, who's more of a cheerful "kissing bandit" than anything else, usually makes a guy settle for passionate kisses (and other foreplay) until he's proven himself worthy of something more intimate.

You should follow suit. If a guy won't wait a month or however long it takes for you to feel comfortable having sex with him, he's just not that into you. Simple as that. If he was, he wouldn't give up so easily. That may be difficult for some of you to believe in light of America's hook-up culture, but guys are just playing the game that so many American women want to play and enjoying it as best they can. You don't have to participate, and you shouldn't if you're looking for a serious relationship.

It's not bitchy to make a guy work and wait for sex. It's smart and strategic, that's all. You need time to get to know who he really is. Once you extend the period out at least a month, the odds of him screwing up increase, and that's not a bad thing. If he does something wrong and unforgivable (e.g., flirting or hooking up with one of your friends, losing his temper, disappearing for a weekend, or otherwise not treating you like a goddess), you'll be glad you didn't close the deal beforehand. So will the next guy who comes along, who may be much more compatible with you.

You can make *rare* exceptions to the longer waiting period if there's sensational chemistry, you're incredibly lonely (or horny), or I'm involved (just kidding! sort of), but otherwise, copy the Latinas, stick to your guns, and make him sweat it out. If you don't think having sex with you is a special event and act accordingly, he won't either.

Hey, if you won't believe me, how about Sherry Argov, author of *Why Men Love Bitches*? She's not right about much, but we agree on this. She advises her readers to keep it platonic with men for the first month and wait as long as possible before having sex.

Even a broken clock is right twice a day.

Principle #6: Show Him That You're Different

This step isn't called "*Tell* Him That You're Different" because actions speak louder than words, and too many American women say meaningless things that guys have learned to ignore, especially on dating websites. If you want men to treat you like a Goddess, you need to *show* them that you're different from other women with a chip on their shoulder, ulterior motives, and heavy baggage out the wazoo. Talk is cheap.

Most Latinas don't have this problem. When an American guy first encounters a *Symmetrical Force* or *Euro-Mina*, for instance, he almost always notices that she's different from the American norm within the first few minutes. It's refreshing and exciting. All bets are off. That works to her advantage.

American women don't get the same benefit of the doubt because most guys have been there and done that too many times. They have a pre-conceived notion that American women are ultimately going to disappoint, reject, fleece, belittle, or otherwise emasculate them. I call it the relationship equivalent of post-traumatic stress syndrome or poor dog training. But don't worry. If you really are different, *you* can snap him out of it, and you can do it in a nice way. There's always a workaround, and there's no need to be a bitch; that would only confirm that you're *not* different from the norm.

Show him that you know how to dress, talk, and act like a woman and enjoy doing so. Show him that you like and respect men. Show him that you're warm, friendly, and approachable but expect to be treated like a Goddess at all times. And show him that you don't use sex to manipulate men or mindlessly sleep with every guy who comes along and survives three dates or less.

Works like a charm … if you're different.

Principle #7: Mind Your Own Business

Men can be difficult. There are some real liars, jerks, slobs, players, and trolls out there. I get it, trust me. I'm not making excuses for them and neither should you. But they shouldn't matter because they're not your problem.

You should be narrowly focused on attracting, getting, and keeping a really *great* guy, and the only way to do that is to mind your own business — physical, mental, emotional, and spiritual — and do things that maximize your likelihood of success with men.

I'm not suggesting that you adopt a bitchy attitude and expect rational guys to accept you as you are — take it or leave it! — even if you're not particularly attractive, desirable, or feminine. That's not minding your own business; that's quitting and letting yourself go. It's what losers do, and it's almost always coupled with male-bashing, whining, and complaining that will make you look even worse. What's the point of putting your nose into everyone else's business when you can't even manage your own?

What if you're minding your own business and being the best you can be and some guy you like comes along who still isn't impressed? That's not your business either. It's his. There's nothing more you can do than your best, and there's no accounting for taste. You may learn something that helps you to attract and get a similar guy next time, and those are valuable lessons, but there's no sense in beating yourself (or him) up over it.

Keep your head up and focus on what you can control *and* improve — your business. There are plenty of eligible bachelors who are looking for a woman who can handle men and life in stride, with a laugh and a smile. It conveys confidence — not bitchiness — and it attracts men. Good ones.

Principle #8: Do the Opposite, If Necessary

What if you apply Principles 1-7 and nothing changes? You still feel like a Ghost out there. You're even starting to wonder whether you should give up and become a full-fledged American bitch like everyone else.

In that case, do "The Opposite."

The Opposite Principle is based on a famous episode of *Seinfeld*, where George Costanza and Jerry Seinfeld had the following exchange:

> George: "My life is the complete opposite of everything I want it to be. Every instinct I have in every aspect of my life, be it something to wear, something to eat … It's often wrong."
>
> Jerry: "If every instinct you have is wrong, then the opposite would have to be right."

George thought that insight was brilliant. All he needed to do to turn his life around was *the exact opposite* of every instinct, habit, tendency or inclination he had at that time.

Then, sure enough, George transformed from a lonely, unemployed loser living with his parents into a magnetic ladies man working as a high-priced executive for the New York Yankees before the 22-minute show was over.

I realize that *Seinfeld* is just a really good TV sitcom, but doing the opposite of whatever you're doing right now may be the shock therapy you need to get out of your rut and open your mind to other alternatives.

Steve Sample, in his bestselling book, *The Contrarian's Guide to Leadership*, offered some similar wisdom about application of the Opposite Principle from a somewhat more authoritative source, Aristotle:

> "Aristotle noted that, when carpenters wish to straighten a warped board, they don't put it in a jip that simply holds it straight; rather they put it in a jig that bends it in the opposite direction from that in which it is warped. After a week or two in this reverse-bending

> configuration, the board naturally springs back to a straight shape when it is released from the jig.
>
> So it is when we attempt to correct our own weaknesses. We must bend over backward in an effort to overcompensate, and in that way we just might achieve a reasonable middle ground."

What does this mean for you? That depends on your current instincts, habits, tendencies and inclinations when it comes to dating and relationships. If you're a bitch who's hoping to change — God bless you — then you've got to act on the opposite of that bitchy impulse for a while, which should make you the sweetest girl in town. If you're highly promiscuous and attracting the wrong kind of guys, it's time to start saying "No" to casual sex.

And yes, if you really are one of those American women who are "too nice" to guys in certain ways — I would call it "too stupid" because I don't see niceness as a liability, but whatever — then you'll have to be a lot more selfish and demanding for a while. Call it bitchier if you want, as long as it works for you. Just don't keep it up for too long. If you don't spring back to a sensible middle ground within a reasonable period of time, you'll defeat the purpose. You can damage your friendships and reputation as well. It's just not worth it. There are already too many American bitches to go around.

Principle #9: Develop Better Habits

In the movie *Grand Canyon*, there's a great scene about how we persevere and forge ahead in the face of hardship. Over breakfast, Simon (Danny Glover) tells Mack (Kevin Kline) about his father's worn, rugged face:

> Simon: When I used to look at that face, and see all the pain there, all the things he lost, all the hurt he had, I wondered why he wanted to go on, why he just didn't lay down and give it up.
>
> Mack: Did you figure it out?
>
> Simon: No. Never figured out much about that guy. I asked him though.
>
> Mack: What did he say?
>
> Simon: Habit.

Good habits don't just help us survive. They increase our likelihood of success in all areas of life and help us to enjoy the journey more as well.

My grandmother Kitty Howe ("Gram"), who was 99 when she passed away a few years ago, was truly delightful. She had aches and pains, stress, anxiety, and other problems like the rest of us, and there were times when she expressed a strong opinion about this or that, but there was always a smile and laugh ready to go. Everyone loved her.

One day, taking a cue from the movie *City Slickers* when Billy Crystal ("Mitch") asks Jack Palance ("Curly") what the one secret to life is, I asked Gram the same question. She giggled and said: "Oh, just be happy and laugh a lot." At first, I was a little disappointed because I expected something more profound. Then it hit me. By thinking and living that way each day, she'd developed a habit of happiness and a great sense of humor. She was habitually happy and cheerful. Not such a bad way to live, is it?

Latinas have developed habits that appeal to American men and make them more likely to be treated like Goddesses, not Ghosts. You can, too. Just keep an eye on the habits you already have, jettison the bad ones, and start developing some new ones that move you in the right direction.

It takes time, but it's worth it.

Principle #10: Train Him Well

According to Jerry Seinfield, "[m]en want the same thing from their underwear that they want from women: a little bit of support, and a little bit of freedom." There's some truth in that statement, as in all good comedy. Men are simple. They're just not *that* simple. You gotta keep an eye on them. And you gotta set some boundaries.

Latinas aren't nearly as demanding as militant feminists, but they don't hesitate to educate their men in a (mostly) loving way about acceptable and unacceptable behavior in a relationship. Even the best guys will (accidentally) step on a landmine once in a while unless you tell them where they're hidden in advance.

What's the best training method?

I can't get into specifics here, but I will recommend a fun little book on the subject: Karen Salmansohn's *How to Make Your Man Behave in 21 Days or Less Using the Secrets of Professional Dog Trainers*. It's an illustrated, tongue-in-cheek guide to training men that, in some simple and amusing ways, isn't far off the mark. Don't take it too seriously, of course; just be clear with your man about what you think and want from him. It's a great way to minimize conflict and avoid (Mars/Venus-type) misunderstandings.

Men are simple, but you need to train them well.

And remember: Even after you go from Ghost to Goddess, the game ain't over. As long as the relationship continues, he'll be taking cues from you.

Make them good ones.

Oh, and don't be a bitch about it.

GHOST TO GODDESS TIPS & INSPIRATION

For more tips on going from Ghost to Goddess, inspiration for your own unique transformation, and access to free book updates,

visit **JoeBovino.com.**

Advice for America's Latinas

Hola, Latinas!

I'd like to close this final chapter by sharing a few thoughts with you.

If you want to attract, get and keep the best American guys even more frequently and successfully than you already do, consider these five friendly suggestions:

1. **Continue Focusing on Your Education and Financial Independence**: Many of you are already relatively well-educated and financially independent. If so, keep it up! If not, get started. A smart Latina with her own money is more appealing than an uneducated one who expects her man to do all of the financial heavy lifting.

2. **Don't Act on Every Jealous Impulse**: American men love your passion when it's channeled in positive directions and appreciate that you care so much about protecting and preserving relationships, but don't let jealousy get the best of you. We all get a little jealous once in a while, but you can score points with American men by not overreacting. I don't know any men who like it when that happens.

3. **Beware of Welfare Benefits and the Cycle of Dependency**: The U.S. government has lured many low-skilled, poorly educated illegal immigrants into the country over the last few years — mainly from Central America and Mexico — with promises of amnesty and welfare. All I want to say about that right now is this: Watch out for welfare benefits. You may need them in the short-term to survive. That's understandable. But welfare has a tendency to trap good people in a cycle of dependency and destroy families who rely on it for too long. You can do better than that. So can your kids.

4. **Beware of Militant Feminists**: America's militant feminists will do whatever it takes - lie, cheat, steal, and smear - to recruit and sign you up for the "cause," such as it is. There's no harm in listening to their hostile messages about (white) men if you want to, but don't let them lead you down a self-destructive path. Follow no one, including me. Think for yourself and apply some common sense. Do what's right and best for YOU.

5. **Learn to Speak English Fluently**: The only thing standing between many of you and *a lot* more American men who'd like to date and marry you is a language barrier. It's true that guys like me should learn to speak Spanish fluently. But you can help yourself and your family in so many ways by studying English. It's the language of business in the United States and, increasingly, the language of love.

Thanks for reading **Why *Latinas* Get the Guy**!

Let's continue the conversation at **JoeBovino.com**.

NOTES

Introduction

Malcolm Gladwell, *Outliers: The Story of Success* (New York: Little, Brown and Company 2008), p. 221.

Helen Smith, PhD, *Men on Strike: Why Men Are Boycotting Marriage, Fatherhood, and the American Dream – and Why It Matters* (Encounter Books, 2013).

Chapter One: KARMA IS A BITCH

Sherry Argov, *Why Men Love Bitches: From Doormat to Dreamgirl – A Woman's Guide to Holding Her Own in a Relationship* (Adams Media, 2009), pgs. xiv, xvi, 6, 9, 14, 17, 19, 20, 23, 44, 50, 57, 61, 69, 73, 99, 112, 116, 123, 146, 185, 212, 216, 230, and 233.

Gigi Engle, "24 Reasons Nice Guys Always Chase The B*tch – As Told By The B*tch," *Elite Daily* (December 16, 2014), http://elitedaily.com/dating/nice-guys-always-chase/882130 (Retrieved January 2, 2015).

Kara Brown, "Watch a Woman Experience 100 Instances of Street Harassment in One Day," *Jezebel* (October 28, 2014), http://jezebel.com/watch-a-woman-experience-100-instances-of-street-harass-165180 (Retrieved December 2, 2014).

Susan Schorn, "How to Kick a Guy in the Balls: An Illustrated Guide," *Jezebel* (November 12, 2014), http://jezebel.com/how-to-kick-a-guy-in-the-balls-an-illustrated-guide-1657810297 (Retrieved December 20, 2014).

Lindy West, "The 92 'Species' of Women According to an Incredibly Stupid Dude from a P90X Video," *Jezebel* (May 8, 2012) http://jezebel.com/5908451/the-92-species-of-women-according-to-one-incredibly-stupid-dude (Retrieved January 2, 2015).

Emma Grey, "Joe Bovino's Field Guide to Chicks May Be Worst Book Ever," *Jezebel* (May 9, 2012), http://www.huffingtonpost.com/emma-gray/joe-bovino-field-guide-to-chicks-of-the-united-states-worst-book-ever_b_1504416.html (Retrieved January 2, 2015).

Charlotte Allen, "Top 10 feminist fiascos of 2014," LA Times (December 19, 2014), http://www.latimes.com/opinion/opinion-la/la-ol-top-10-feminist-fiascoes-of-2014-20141219-story.html#page=1 (Retrieved January 2, 2015).

Reannon Muth, "No Sex in the City: What It's Like to Be Single and Foreign in Japan," *Vagabondish* (March 5, 2013), http://www.vagabondish.com/female-foreign-japan (Retrieved January 2, 2015).

Reannon Muth, "Are North American Women Really THAT Bad," *Taken By The Wind*, http://www.takenbythewind.com/2010/09/17/are-north-american-women-really-that-bad (Retrieved January 5, 2015).

Chapter Two: JANE, YOU IGNORANT SLUT

"Jane, you ignorant slut," Saturday Night Live Clip, 1975 (Point Counterpoint Lee Marvin and Michele Triola), *IMDB* http://www.imdb.com/video/hulu/vi119734297 (Retrieved January 3, 2015).

Dossie Easton and Janet W. Hardy, *The Ethical Slut: A Practical Guide to Polyamory, Open Relationships and Other Adventures* (Celestial Arts, 2009).

Chapter Three: AMERICA'S LATINAS

Samuel P. Huntington, *The Clash of Civilizations and the Remaking of World Order* (Simon & Schuster Paperbacks, 1996), p. 20.

Malcolm Gladwell, *Outliers: The Story of Success* (New York: Little, Brown and Company 2008), p. 221.

Taco Belle

Jada Yuan, "Belle Curves: Sara Ramirez," *New York Magazine* (September 18, 2006). http://nymag.com/arts/tv/reviews/21334/ (Retrieved May 10, 2010).

"Mexican Ancestry Maps," *Epodunk.com.* http://www.epodunk.com/ancestry/Mexican.html (Retrieved November 25, 2014).

"List of Mexican Americans," *Wikipedia, the Free Encyclopedia* http://en.wikipedia.org/wiki/List_of_Mexican_Americans (Retrieved November 25, 2014).

Bumbshell

H.J., "Brazilians: Portuguese for the perplexed," *The Economist* (May 24, 2013), http://www.economist.com/blogs/johnson/2013/05/brazilians (Retrieved January 4, 2014).

H.J., "Brazilians, ctd: More Perplexing Portuguese," *The Economist* (June 4, 2013), http://www.economist.com/blogs/johnson/2013/06/brazilians-ctd (Retrieved January 4, 2014).

"Brazilian Ancestry Maps," *Epodunk.com.* http://www.epodunk.com/ancestry/Brazilian.html (Retrieved November 25, 2014).

"List of Brazilian Americans," *Wikipedia, the Free Encyclopedia* http://en.wikipedia.org/wiki/List_of_Brazilian_Americans (Retrieved on November 25, 2014).

Euro-Mina

James Bracken, *Che Boludo! A gringo's guide to understanding the Argentines*, Editorial Caleuche (2005).

"Argentine American," *Wikipedia, The Free Encyclopedia.* http://en.wikipedia.org/wiki/Argentine_American (Retrieved February 3, 2012).

"List of Argentine Americans," *Wikipedia, the Free Encyclopedia* http://en.wikipedia.org/wiki/List_of_Argentine_Americans (Retrieved November 25, 2014).

Symmetrical Force

"Colombian Ancestry Maps," *Epodunk.com*. http://www.epodunk.com/ancestry/Colombian.html (Retrieved November 25, 2014).

"List of Colombian Americans," *Wikipedia, the Free Encyclopedia* http://en.wikipedia.org/wiki/List_of_Colombian_Americans (Retrieved November 25, 2014).

La Guitarra

"Puerto Ricans in the United States," *Wikipedia, The Free Encyclopedia* (graphic by Angelo Falcón, Puerto Rican Population in the United States, 2000). http://en.wikipedia.org/wiki/Puerto_Ricans_in_the_United_States (Retrieved November 25, 2014).

"Puerto Rican Migration Patterns 1995-2000," *Wikipedia, The Free Encyclopedia* (graphic by Angelo Falcón). http://en.wikipedia.org/wiki/File:PR_Migration_1995-2000.jpg (Retrieved November 25, 2014).

"List of Stateside Puerto Ricans," *Wikipedia, the Free Encyclopedia* http://en.wikipedia.org/wiki/List_of_Stateside_Puerto_Ricans (Retrieved November 26, 2014).

Nuyorican

Movieline, October 1996.

"Jennifer Lopez: 'Skinny Girls Miss Out'" (citing quote to *New York Post*), *US Weekly* (January 8, 2010). http://www.usmagazine.com/healthylifestyle/news/jennifer-lopez-skinny-girls-miss-out-201081 (Retrieved May 10, 2010).

See also "Jennifer Lopez," *AskMen*; http://www.askmen.com/celebs/women/singer/3_jennifer_lopez.html (Retrieved May 10, 2010).

"List of Stateside Puerto Ricans," *Wikipedia, the Free Encyclopedia* http://en.wikipedia.org/wiki/List_of_Stateside_Puerto_Ricans (Retrieved November 26, 2014).

"Nuyorican," *Wikipedia, The Free Encyclopedia.* http://en.wikipedia.org/wiki/Nuyorican (Retrieved May 10, 2010).

"Puerto Rican Migration Patterns 1995-2000," *Wikipedia, The Free Encyclopedia* (graphic by Angelo Falcón). http://en.wikipedia.org/wiki/File: PR_Migration_1995-2000.jpg (Retrieved August 17, 2010).

Trifecta

"Venezuelan Ancestry Maps," *Epodunk.com*. http://www.epodunk.com/ancestry/Venezuelan.html (Retrieved April 17, 2010).

"List of Venezuelan Americans," *Wikipedia, the Free Encyclopedia* http://en.wikipedia.org/wiki/List_of_Venezuelan_Americans (Retrieved November 26, 2014).

Transformer

"Cuban Ancestry Maps," *Epodunk.com.* http://www.epodunk.com/ancestry/Cuban.html (Retrieved Noevermber 26, 2014).

"List of Cuban Americans," *Wikipedia, the Free Encyclopedia* http://en.wikipedia.org/wiki/List_of_Cuban_Americans (Retrieved November 26, 2014).

Cinnamon Swirl

"Central America and Caribbean: Dominican Republic," *The World Factbook,* Central Intelligence Agency. https://www.cia.gov/library/publications/the-world-factbook/geos/dr.html (Retrieved May 10, 2010).

Beauty Call

David Katz, "Zoe Saldana: A Woman We Love," *Esquire* (May 2009), p. 92–95.

"Dominican Ancestry Maps," *Epodunk.com.* http://www.epodunk.com/ancestry/Dominican-Republic.html (Retrieved April 17, 2010).

Perusian

"Peruvian Ancestry Maps," *Epodunk.com.* http://www.epodunk.com/ancestry/Dominican-Republic.html (Retrieved April 17, 2010).

Pupusa

Jeremy Mumford, "Salvadoran Americans," *Everyculture.com* (Advameg, Inc., 2008). http://www.everyculture.com/multi/Pa-Sp/Salvadoran-Americans.html (Retrieved May 10, 2010).

"Salvadoran Ancestry Maps," *Epodunk.com.* http://www.epodunk.com/ancestry/Salvadoran.html (Retrieved April 17, 2010).

Ecuadorable

"Ecuadorian Ancestry Maps," *Epodunk.com.* http://www.epodunk.com/ancestry/Ecuadorian.html (Retrieved May 10, 2010).

Hotemalan

"Guatemalan Ancestry Maps," *Epodunk.com.* http://www.epodunk.com/ancestry/Guatemalan.html (Retrieved May 10, 2010).

Chapter Four: AMERICAN WOMEN

Malcolm Gladwell, *Outliers: The Story of Success* (New York: Little, Brown and Company 2008), p. 221.

49er

"Freeboobing," *Urbandictionary.com.* http://www.urbandictionary.com/define.php?term=freeboobing (Retrieved January 5, 2012).

"Going Solo in the USA," *Sperling's BestPlaces.* http://www.bestplaces.net/docs/studies/SoloCities.aspx, for percentages and ratios of single men and women (ages 25–64) in the U.S. (Retrieved May 8, 2010).

Sili-Clone

"Map of Orange County Beaches," *Lonelyplanet.com.* http://www.lonelyplanet.com/maps/north-america/usa/orangecounty- beaches (Retrieved May 8, 2010).

Perfect 6

"America's Best (and Worst) Cities for Dating," *Sperling's BestPlaces.* http://www.bestplaces.net/docs/studies/DatingCities.aspx (Retrieved May 8, 2010).

Hurt Rocker

"The Emo Hangout," *Emo Corner.* http://www.emo-corner.com/emo-girls-pictures (Retrieved April 27, 2010).

Uncyclopedia, *Emo,* http://uncyclopedia.wikia.com/wiki/Emo (Retrieved May 8, 2010).

"How to Get an Emo Girlfriend," *wikiHow.* http://www.wikihow.com/Get-an-Emo-Girlfriend (Retrieved May 8, 2010).

"Straight Edge," *Wikipedia, The Free Encyclopedia.* http://en.wikipedia.org/wiki/Straight_edge (Retrieved May 8, 2010).

Brooding Barfly

For a more in-depth analysis of hipster subculture, see Brenna Ehrlich and Andrea Bartz, *Stuff Hipsters Hate: A Field Guide To The Passionate Opinions Of The Indifferent* (Ulysses Press, 2010), and Robert Lanham, *The Hipster Handbook* (First Anchor Books Edition, February 2003). I relied on each of these books for insights into the subculture.

"How to Be a Hipster," *wikiHow.* http://www.wikihow.com/Be-a-Hipster (Retrieved September 20, 2011).

"Hipster," *Urbandictionary.com.* http://www.urbandictionary.com/define.php?term=hipster (Retrieved September 23, 2011).

Big Bang

"Mississippi is the fattest state for the 9th straight year, Colorado still leanest, Arkansas getting fatter, Hawaii slimmer," *CalorieLab.com* (United States of Obesity 2014). http://calorielab.com/news/2014/05/05/fattest-states-2014/ (Retrieved January 3, 2015).

Michelle Fox, "America's fattest cities," *CNBC.com.* http://bit.ly/KBeGdA (March 28, 2012).

Flegal, KM, Carroll, MD, Ogden, CL, Curtin, LR. "Prevalence and Trends in Obesity Among US Adults, 1999–2008," *Journal of the American Medical Association* (2010), pp. 235–241.

"F as in Fat: How Obesity Policies Are Failing In America," *Trust for America's Health and Robert Wood Johnson Foundation, Issue Report* (July 2009). http://healthyamericans.org/reports/obesity2009/ (Retrieved May 8, 2010).

"hippocampus," *Urbandictionary.com.* http://www.urbandictionary.com/define.php?term=hippocampus&defid=4367825 (Retrieved January 4, 2012).

Cougar

College Times. http://collegetimes.us/top-5-cougar-towns (Retrieved September 9, 2011).

Chapter Five: THE GHOST TO GODDESS PRINCIPLES

Kristen Houghton, "The New Trophy Wife," Huff Post Women (December 13, 2014), http://www.huffingtonpost.com/kristen-houghton/the-new-trophy-wife_b_6207364.html (Retrieved December 19, 2014).

Amanda Chatel, "11 Pretty Cool Things You Didn't Know About Flirting," *Yahoo Style* (January 3, 2015) https://www.yahoo.com/style/11-pretty-cool-things-you-didnt-know-about-106616804873.html (Retrieved January 3, 2015).

Joe Bovino, *Field Guide to Chicks of the United States* (Chickspotting, LLC, 2012), pgs. 147 and 167.

Rob Asghar, "Do The Opposite: Seinfeldian Wisdom For A Brighter New Year," *Forbes* (December 30, 2013), http://www.forbes.com/sites/robasghar/2013/12/30/do-the-opposite-seinfeldian-wisdom-for-a-brighter-new-year (Retrieved January 7, 2015).

Steven P. Sample, *The Contrarian's Guide to Leadership* (Jossey-Bass 2003).

Karen Salmansohn's *How to Make Your Man Behave in 21 Days or Less Using the Secrets of Professional Dog Trainers*, (Workman Publishing Company, 1994).

CREDITS

BOOK DESIGN

Rick Soldin (book-comp.com) provided book design and page layout services.

Dr. Jay Polmar of iPublicidades (https://www.elance.com/s/speedread) provided print-on-demand and cover design services.

ILLUSTRATIONS

Linda Jackson and **Darren Jackson** of DarlinDesign (darlindesign.co.uk) provided the following illustrations: Beauty Call, Boca Bitch, Bumbshell, Ecuadorable, Euro-Mina, Hotemalan, La Guitarra, Parts of a Chica, Perusian, Pupusa, So Ho', Taco Belle, and the Latina illustration on the front cover.

Carsten Mell (carstenmell.com) provided the following illustrations: 49er, Bigger Better Deal, Big Bang, Cinnamon Swirl, Cougar, Hurt Rocker, Nuyorican, Perfect 6, Sili-Clone, South Beeotch, Symmetrical Force, Transformer, and Trifecta.

Gerben den Heeten of Gerb-Art (gerb-art.com) provided the Brooding Barfly illustration.

Christine Orvis (cm-imagingstudio.com) retouched the following illustrations: Brooding Barfly, Perusian, Symmetrical Force, and Transformer.

ACKNOWLEDGMENTS

A special thank you is owed to my incredible family and friends who helped me get this book over the finish line, especially Mike Kim, Bryan Christy, Priya Krishnamurthy, Rachel Hamm Gertz, Greg Centineo, Gary Ghiaey, and fellow authors from Mike Koenigs' Publish and Profit group, especially Walter Terry, Jason P. Jordan, Melissa Risdon, and Justine Malalis Gronwald.

Thanks as well to the following individuals who supported me in this endeavor, in one way or another, along the way:

Arabella Carey Adolfsson, Lefer Ayala, Tyler Barth, Lisa M. Beegle, Giselle A. Blanco, Sandra Blanco-Fisher, Ori Blumenfeld, Todd Bobo, Simon Bonello, Maria Bonvy, Jerry Bovino, Pat Burns, Karina Call-Costa, Pamela Canellas, Shannon Carney, Xin Chung, Wendy J. Cury, Irene Tomo Cooper, Jossie Cordoba, Paul Crespo, Cristina Michel Cruz, Nancy Cruz, Claudia Del Rosario, Dario Desrouleaux, Florencia Martinez Echenique, Diana Ecker, Yamilet Escobar, Fadi Essmaeel, Tanya L. Fox, Martin Emilio Garavaglia, Jeanette Garcia, Alexandra Montalvo Garibaldi, Kahlelah Goodine, Corin Cartegena Grillo, Jose Guerrero, Diana Guido, Fernanda Hedmont, Veronica Herrera, Noelia Sanchez Bravo Herrera, Marie Beal Hutchison, Bryan Jardine, Luz Adriana Jimenez, Evelyn Jimenez, Susan Johnston, Hal Juhl, Gigi Magalong, Cindy Martinez, Iris Matos, Kim Matuka, Margaret Matuka, Kiki Monsterly, Paula Munevar-Kordi, Brian Olea, Erick Padilla, Gil Patino, Loretta Pena-Vasquez, Yolanda Peraza, Daisy Pino, Nancy Pinto, Juan Pablo Raba, Hope Radar, Parker Randal, Alex Rivera, Laeticia Rodriguez, Jamee Ruth, Kerly Sanchez, Gleicy Santos, Luciana Scarabello, Carolina Schwartz, Howie Simon, Sam Sloves, Debra Young Stearns, Noelia Suarez, Lisa Song Sutton, Mia Tabares, Caroline Taicher, Marc Valdiviezo, Ingrid Vaynovsky, Silvia Villagran, and Ilca Monique Lorenzo Wanderley.

CONCLUSION

NOT SO FAST, AMIGOS!

Sign up for access to free no-BS dating and relationship advice, training videos, livecasts, and other resources as soon as they're released.

Visit **JoeBovino.com.**

Later, Bitches!

(Just kidding … but I do hope to see you later.)

ABOUT THE AUTHOR

APPEARANCE: Looks like the guy in the photo if the light hits him just right. Relatively fit and healthy for a guy who spends way too much time staring at a laptop.

SONG: Known to channel Dean Martin, Frank Sinatra or Michael Bublé at karaoke clubs with varying degrees of success. Tried to do the same with Tom Jones once and won't make that mistake again.

BEHAVIOR: Lawyer turned three-time #1 bestselling author and virtual field guide. Appears as a cast member in the original P90X workout program and continues to workout regularly. Loves his best friends like brothers but won't let them borrow his car or his girl. Enjoys international business, cross-cultural affairs (in various forms), history, politics and satire. Dances better than your average gringo.

MATING: Loves women more than Fabio. More player-coach than player these days. Master of international relations. (Well, not exactly, but he does have a master's degree in international relations from the University of Southern California.) Loyal and ready to settle down but prepared to stay single if necessary, at least until he's too old to feed himself. Gold medalist in bed, no matter what she says.

MAGNETS: Prefers extraordinary women (who love his books and think he's awesome) to ordinary ones (who don't). No mustache is a plus. Irritable bowel syndrome is a deal-breaker.

LOCATION: Born and raised in Cherry Hill, New Jersey. Attended college in scenic Charlottesville, Virginia and graduate school in Los Angeles. Spent most of the last twenty years in California (mostly Los Angeles) and Florida (mostly Miami and Delray Beach) but travels often for business and pleasure.

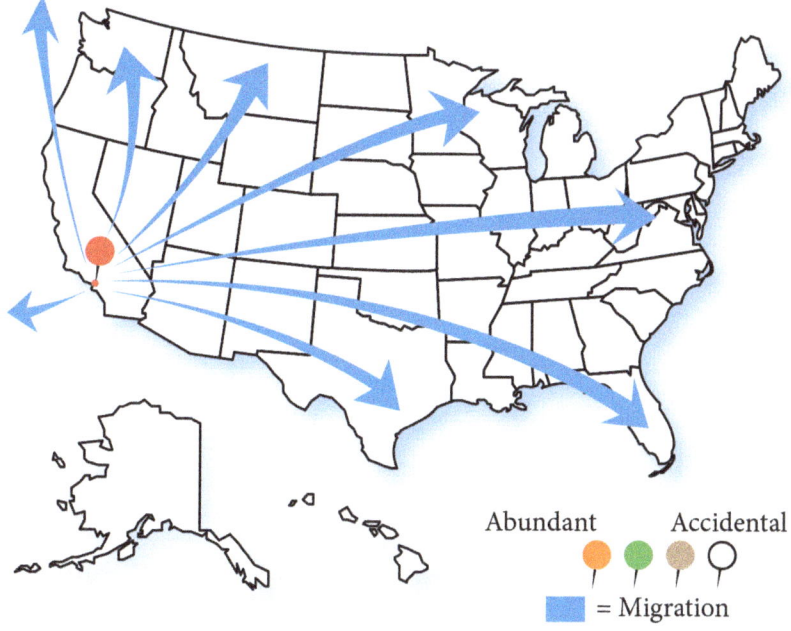

MIGRATION: Frequent flyer.

Follow Joe on Twitter @joebovino, join him on Facebook (joebovinopage), and visit his website at JoeBovino.com.

www.ingramcontent.com/pod-product-compliance
Lightning Source LLC
Chambersburg PA
CBHW040334300426
44113CB00021B/2746